THE JOY OF
Chocolate

JUDITH OLNEY

BARRON'S

New York • London • Toronto • Sydney

All inquiries should be addressed to:
Barron's Educational Series, Inc.
250 Wireless Boulevard
Hauppauge, New York 11788

Library of Congress Catalog No. 82-11356

Cloth Edition
International Standard Book No. 0-8120-5435-0

Paper Edition
International Standard Book No. 0-8120-4279-4

Library of Congress Cataloging in Publication Data

Olney, Judith.
      The joy of chocolate.
      Includes index.
      1. Cookery (Chocolate) I. Klingel, Ruth. II Title.
TX767.C5046 1982   641.6'3374   82-11356
ISBN 0-8120-4279-4 (pbk)
ISBN 0-8120-5435-0

Credits

Photography:
      Matthew Klein, color photographs
      Silver platter for Cheesecake courtesy of Georg Jensen
      Silversmiths. All other table settings courtesy of James
      Robinson Inc./James II Galleries Inc.

Jacket and cover design: Milton Glaser, Inc.

Book design: Milton Glaser, Inc.

PRINTED AND BOUND IN HONG KONG

01 4900 9876543

Contents

Preface

When I began composing recipes for *The Joy of Chocolate,* I must admit that even as a confirmed "chocoholic," I worried about the monotony of dealing with one subject, one ingredient, for such a long and intense period. Now as I write this, after having tested the recipes and having become deeply acquainted with the substance, I know that there is no other ingredient in cooking so versatile, so exciting to work and create with as chocolate.

In the course of preparing the chocolate recipes in this book, I melted it, formed it, shaped it, and chocolate expanded to airy thinness in omelets or contracted to solid forms in molds and candies. I curled it, grated it, scraped it, and chocolate melted into hot sustaining liquid, mounted into thick rich sauces, or froze into cold solid creams. I played with it, and chocolate turned to delicious joyful fantasies in my hands. There was, quite simply, nothing I asked of chocolate that it could not do.

I came to know chocolate as a distinct personality, with almost as many foibles and traits as any living creature. (If, for instance, chocolate has a gender, I am convinced it must be feminine, for certainly it demands to be treated and handled with all the respect due a temperamental *grande dame.*) And in looking at the recipes in this book, I am struck by how much they tell of the personality, the symbolic character, the very history of chocolate.

The story of the cocoa bean, its discovery in the New World by Columbus and Cortes and the subsequent craze for chocolate that swept Europe in the sixteenth century, have been documented countless times, but it is for us to realize that we pay homage to that exotic history whenever we combine spices with chocolate (as in this book's chocolate curry, frozen Mexican chocolate, cinnamon-spiced cookies); and whenever we drink a frothy brew of steaming homemade chocolate from a mug. (For two hundred years, hot liquid chocolate was the only form in which chocolate was consumed.)

Because chocolate came from the unknown New World, because it stimulated and refreshed, it was considered by many in the first centuries of its Western consumption to be an aphrodisiac, a potent stimulant to love. (Casanova is supposed to have consumed gallons of the stuff.) Today those assumptions still linger in more symbolic ways. Though we do not consider chocolate an aphrodisiac, it still remains a sure sign of romance and esteem, from the heart-shaped offerings of chocolate creams on St. Valentine's Day, to the courting suitor's gift of sweetmeats to his love. (And perhaps there is no greater gustatory symbol of self-love than to indulge oneself unabashedly in a glorious box of chocolates.) In this book, romantic chocolate blossoms in rose-flavored bavarians twined with chocolate ivy, the flowerlike chocolate raspberry torte, and the perfumed orange-flower ice cream with bittersweet chocolate bits. Ah. Is not *bittersweet* a fitting word, one which poets of love and purveyors of candy both find apt?

Chocolate has even more complexity of character, for it is at the same time a symbol of wickedness and guilt (witness all those "Chocolate Decadences," those "Chocolate Sins" tempting us from the pages of food magazines), and a symbol of healthful living (many a candy bar makes its advertising persuasion the fact that chocolate will energize, will revitalize the eater at midday and hold him or her till suppertime). And lately chocolate has become a symbol of exclusive chic, with famous people bringing out their own collections. (For a taste of the rich life, try this book's Designer Brownies.) Many a chocolate maker is finding that pure, high-quality chocolate sells in all sorts of shapes and forms, from chocolate frames to shapely legs, from a set of milk chocolate golf balls to dark chocolate sardines. One only has to fantasize, and chocolate can turn the fantasy into delicious reality. (With this book you can create the giant Chocolate Cabbage Cake filled with luscious whipped cream; a chocolate sack spilling fruit and apricot pudding; amusing white chocolate "ravioli" with dark chocolate hazelnut centers.)

To whatever use you wish to put chocolate, this book will serve. So whip up a batch of chocolate chip cookies; or bake yourself a mile-high devil's food cake, frost it generously, be sure to lick your fingers, and enjoy . . . joy . . . joy *The Joy of Chocolate*.

Acknowledgments

*T*hanks to Kit Crow, Gertrude Lenzer, Kathy Long, Dawn McKinney, Bill Neal, Kate Tresolini, my editor Carole Berglie, and especially Betty Wall.

Chocolate and Other Ingredients

This book was tested with the following specifics:

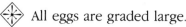 All eggs are graded large.

All cream is heavy cream (which frequently has a higher percentage of butterfat than creams designated as "whipping cream").

The flour is all-purpose, sifted before measuring unless otherwise noted.

All unsweetened, semisweet, and chips are chocolate made by Hershey's. Plain cocoa is Hershey's unless designated as Dutch-process, in which case Droste's cocoa is used. Couverture chocolate is Peters Dark Coating Chocolate, made by the Nestlé Company. Bittersweet and extra-bittersweet chocolate is Tobler. White chocolate is Tobler's Narcisse or Peters White Coating Chocolate.

Substitutions are possible in all instances, but you may want to experiment a little first, especially with different brands of chocolate, since they vary in the percentages of cocoa butter.

Working with Chocolate

*I*n this book I tried to incorporate as much chocolate essence within each recipe as possible. Many of these dishes contain more chocolate per item than do other recipes for similar dishes. Sometimes I increased taste by adding cocoa or by substituting a square or two of unsweetened chocolate for semisweet, or sometimes by exchanging bittersweet chocolate for semisweet. At other times I simply increased chocolate to the maximum a dish could hold and, in so doing, the dish became denser, more fudgelike, moister. In such dishes as mousses, ice creams, and pie fillings any of these methods will work to increase the chocolate quantity and essence. In baking, however, one should observe the following rules for substituting and changing chocolates:

 1 ounce of unsweetened chocolate is equal to 3 tablespoons of cocoa and 1 tablespoon of fat. When you wish to increase cocoa in a cake, you must also increase proportionately the amount of fat and decrease minutely the amount of flour in any given recipe.

 Unsweetened chocolate can be made into semisweet chocolate by adding 1 tablespoon of sugar to each melted ounce. Three ounces of unsweetened chocolate plus 3 tablespoons of sugar equal 4 ounces of semisweet chocolate.

Bittersweet chocolate can be substituted for semisweet chocolate in any recipe. The resulting change is one of flavor only.

When chocolate seems too "sweet" within a recipe (or again, simply to intensify chocolate essence), the sweetness can be rectified by adding a small pinch of cinnamon or instant coffee powder. Both of these substances are bitter, and if they are used in minute quantity, the chocolate essence will intensify, the sweetness will be cut, and neither cinnamon nor coffee will be detectable within the dish.

MELTING CHOCOLATE

Here is where chocolate shows its *grande dame* character. Overheat it the least bit, or have a drop of water in the bowl in which chocolate melts, and chocolate will make a disastrous scene. It will clutch and tighten, stiffen and harden before your very eyes, and refuse to cooperate any further. To rescue chocolate from its obstinacy, try pouring a little oil on the troubled waters (so to speak). For every ounce of chocolate, add around 1 teaspoon of vegetable oil or melted shortening, and beat vigorously until the chocolate behaves itself. Proceed with your recipe.

To melt chocolate with best results, place chocolate in a small pan in a double boiler, or arrange the small pan inside a larger pan containing hot but nowhere near boiling water (this is called a *bain-marie*). Make sure the pan holding the chocolate is completely dry.

Melt the chocolate slowly, then stir until smooth and proceed with the recipe. Here are some other tips:

 If chocolate is to be melted with water or milk or butter, the process is faster and can be done directly over very low heat if you stir it and watch it the whole time.

 The more additives a chocolate has (sugar, milk solids, lecithin, etc.), the more difficult it can be to melt properly. German's sweet chocolate and milk chocolate should be melted over warm water very slowly, and I often grate them first to speed the melting.

 White chocolate (which, according to the F.D.A., is not even chocolate for it contains no cocoa liquor), always seems the most difficult to work with. Its characteristics vary greatly among brands. To assure even melting, always grate white chocolate first (firm the chocolate in the freezer briefly if it is at all soft). The grating is worth the effort, for it allows low heat to melt the small flakes more rapidly. If white chocolate tightens, add a small amount of boiling water and the chocolate will often smooth itself.

 Adding alcohol to chocolate, in liquors or even in vanilla extract, can sometimes cause chocolate to tighten. Smooth by adding melted shortening.

SHAPING CHOCOLATE

Grated Chocolate: For small amounts, I find it easiest to scrape or grate chocolate by simply cutting it finely with a large chef's knife. For a very large amount of chocolate, you might want to use a food processor with a grating blade, but this always seems a bother to clean. If you are at all handy with a knife, that is almost as fast and much neater. The small blade of a Moulijulienne grater will also grate firm, cold chocolate fairly well.

Chocolate Curls: Melt semisweet or couverture chocolate and pour it onto a flat surface, preferably a marble slab though a large Formica counter or cutting board will do. Using a long, thin pastry spatula, spread the chocolate backward and forward until it is a very thin, even layer. Keep working the spatula over the chocolate until the gloss dulls and the chocolate looks as if it is beginning to dry at the edges. Start at the edge. Holding the blade of the spatula at a 45-degree angle, scrape and push against the drying chocolate until it gathers into large curls and rough, barklike pieces (as in those pictured on the Baumkuchen, page 72). Let the pieces dry until firm, then use them as decoration. These may be stored in an airtight container and kept in a cool place.

Chocolate Flakes: Melt chocolate and spread it on a marble slab as in the instructions for chocolate curls. Let the chocolate completely harden, then scrape against it with a knife or spatula and it will flake into thin shavings.

Working with Cream

*A*lways buy the heaviest cream you can find. To whip cream, have the cream well chilled. (Place it in the freezer briefly, especially in hot weather.) Especially in hot weather it is also wise to whip the cream in a chilled bowl placed over ice cubes in a still larger bowl. For small amounts of cream, I find a large balloon whisk works almost as rapidly as an electric mixer and gives me slightly more volume.

When cream is to be sweetened and flavored, whip it until it has thickened first, then gradually start adding sugar and taste the cream until the desired sweetness is reached. I prefer to use confectioners' sugar when sweetening cream; its 3 percent cornstarch addition often helps stabilize cream and keep it from watering, whereas granulated sugar, with its large water content, tends to melt into the cream and speed the separation process.

After the cream is sweetened, flavor it to taste with vanilla or liquor. I prefer an unsweetened cream on rich desserts, a sweet, sugary cream against bitter chocolate dishes.

To prepare cream for mousses and bavarians, beat it only until thickened but not stiff. The more air incorporated into the cream, the drier the final pudding or mousse will be. It is better to slightly underwhip cream when a rich, compact texture is desired in a dish.

For ice creams, do not whip the cream at all. Let the ice cream machine do it, and you will have a lovely, dense texture.

Working with Eggs

*E*ggs separate best when they are cold. The yolk, which is composed largely of fat, is more solidified when cold, less apt to break.

After separating eggs, store extra yolks in a glass container and cover the yolks with oil. They will keep a week this way. Store extra egg whites in the freezer. Freeze each white separately in an ice cube container, then turn out the cubes and keep them in a plastic container in the freezer. You will have exact amounts when necessary.

If a recipe calls for eggs or egg whites at room temperature and you have forgotten to set them out, simply crack the eggs into a bowl and warm them slightly over gentle heat. Stir the eggs with your hand, and you will feel when they become thoroughly warmed.

Recipes call for eggs at room temperature because egg whites mount into a greater volume when they are slightly warm and can incorporate air more readily. In a dish that is dependent on eggs for volume (as in soufflés and sponge cakes), everything you can do to increase volume is worth your effort. Here are some other tips:

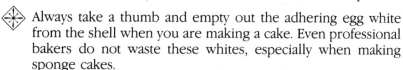 Always take a thumb and empty out the adhering egg white from the shell when you are making a cake. Even professional bakers do not waste these whites, especially when making sponge cakes.

To beat egg whites by hand, place whites in an impeccably clean bowl (preferably a large copper bowl). Roll a large balloon whisk back and forth briefly between the palms of the hands to "break" the whites up, then begin whisking in slow, steady manner, either lifting the whisk around the bowl and out of the eggs or stirring the whisk back and forth against the bowl and always in contact with it. When the whites have thickened and stiffened but still maintain a glossy sheen, and when the whisk is lifted from the bowl and the whites hold up in a smooth peaked mass on top of the whisk, they are ready. Do a very rapid, hard whisk two or three times around the bowl to "tighten" the whites, then proceed with the recipe.

 If beaten egg whites are to be folded into a cake batter in a sponge or pound cake, mix one third of the recipe's sugar tablespoon by tablespoon with the whites toward the end of their beating. The stiff, marshmallowlike whites that result will fold into a batter much more smoothly than plain whites.

 To fold beaten egg whites into a batter, pour the lighter mixture (usually the eggs), on top of the heavier mixture in a rounded bowl. Using your hands (preferably) or a rubber spatula, cut down through the mixtures to the bottom of the bowl, then lift up and turn your hand or spatula at the same time. Continue cutting through the mixtures gently but rapidly (turn the bowl with your other hand), until both mixtures are well mixed. Do not overwork, as you want the quantity of air beaten into the eggs to remain as voluminous as possible. Never mind if there is an occasional speck of whites not incorporated.

Equipment

*T*he following pieces of equipment seem to me the best and most necessary for professional results in working with chocolate:

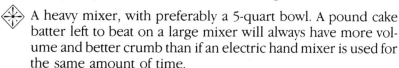

A heavy mixer, with preferably a 5-quart bowl. A pound cake batter left to beat on a large mixer will always have more volume and better crumb than if an electric hand mixer is used for the same amount of time.

A food processor. Most useful for chopping and grinding nuts. An easy method to melt chocolate is to place grated chocolate in the bowl of a processor, turn on the processor, then pour in a small amount of boiling water through the feed tube—instant smooth, melted chocolate.

Scrapers and spatulas. An assortment of rubber-tipped spatulas both large and small and—for chocolate curls and spreading frosting evenly—a long, flexible metal pastry spatula. A stainless-steel pastry scraper for cleaning counters is a must.

Candy thermometer. A heavy glass thermometer is useful for registering sugar syrup and fudge temperatures. It gives more predictable results than dripping syrup off spoons into cold water.

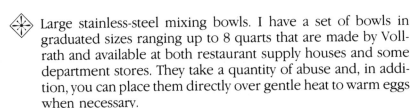 Large stainless-steel mixing bowls. I have a set of bowls in graduated sizes ranging up to 8 quarts that are made by Vollrath and available at both restaurant supply houses and some department stores. They take a quantity of abuse and, in addition, you can place them directly over gentle heat to warm eggs when necessary.

Heavy baking trays. Preferably these should be made from cast iron; they will not warp in the oven, and they will protect delicate items from scorching better than thin aluminum sheets. They also have raised edges, and trays without that protection are often useless.

Pastry bags. Several large bags, 15 inches long, seem the best for all-purpose uses. (Have one larger bag if you do much meringue work, and one smaller bag for decorative frostings.) The best bags are canvas on the exterior and plastic lined on the interior, or all nylon for easy cleaning. I find large rosette tubes, with their casual swirls of decorative creams, the most useful nozzles. Have a smaller rosette tube for border piping, and several sizes of plain round tubes for piping meringue, and so forth.

Brandied Chocolate Bavarian in a Chocolate Soufflé Dish, pages 2 and 174

Using a Pastry Bag

*T*o fill and use a large pastry bag, fit the bag with the desired tube. If the substance to be piped is at all loose and runny, hold the bag in the left hand with the tip bent upward, the bag pressed against the tube so no filling can enter it. (Or place the bag in a large bowl, with the tip turned up against the side of the bowl.) Fill the bag around half full, and pleat the empty top fabric together neatly. Twist the top of the bag slightly and force out any air bubbles trapped in the bag. Pipe out a small section of frosting to see that it is piping cleanly, then press out designs.

A PAPER PIPING BAG

For fine script lines of frosting or chocolate, it is easiest to make and use paper piping bags. Most kitchen equipment stores carry parchment paper triangles that are 12 by 12 by 16½ inches. (Or you can buy a roll of parchment paper and cut shapes to size.) To make a paper cone, lay the triangle on a counter in front of you (see drawing) with the long end (a–c) at the bottom. (The center of the long end will become the tip of the paper piping bag.) Bring the left point (point a) up, twist it under, and curve the point to meet the top (point b) of the triangle. Bring the right hand point (point c) up and over, and twist it around to the back to meet the top of the triangle and the other two points. All three points will now fit together, and a sharply pointed cone end will be opposite them. Fold the points down and together in three or four places, so they remain stable, then fill the bag no more than half full, and twist the top paper closed. Cut off the pointed tip of the cone with scissors, and gently press the contents to form designs. Particularly with messy chocolate work, it is easier to throw a paper cone away than to have to wash a permanent pastry bag.

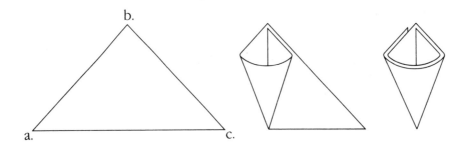

Some Random Thoughts

 When working with chocolate, always wear brown.

 When dipping and coating candies, take the lazy person's way out. Simply brush them over with melted chocolate. The look is more rustic, more distinctive, and your chocolate coating will be thicker.

 Cakes ice best if they sit overnight first, but glazes and icings help a cake retain freshness. If the exterior of a freshly baked cake to be frosted seems loose of crumb, spread it over gently with very soft butter, then place the cake in the freezer to harden. The frosting or glaze will adhere to the smooth surface and pick up no crumbs in the process.

 An old-fashioned method to test cakes for doneness is simply to take the cake from the oven, put it up to your ear, and listen to it. Cooked cakes make no noise; still damp ones tend to sound rather spitty.

 Always cool cakes on a rack to keep their bottoms from becoming overmoist.

 Have a cake baking and forget the time it's due out of the oven? The first point at which you actually smell the cake should give you a clue that it is about done. Unlike yeasted bread, cake batter does not put out an aroma until it actually becomes a firm cake.

 To grease and flour baking trays, rub the surface of the tray over with oil or shortening (use fingers or wax paper). Run a generous scoop of flour along the top narrow edge of the tray, then slant the tray up and give it a good tap on the counter. The flour will slide neatly, smoothly-down in just the right amount, with the excess falling off onto the counter. If you do a large amount of baking, use this professional trick. Mix 1 cup of shortening with 1 cup of flour. Store in the shortening can and simply scoop out a portion with a folded piece of wax paper and rub over the baking tray.

 Place soufflés and sponge cakes (indeed, anything that rises from the expansion of eggs) in their dishes on a cookie sheet. This helps diffuse uneven heat so that dishes rise straight and even.

 Most ovens have hot spots. Know the heating capacity of your oven intimately, and guard against overbrowning by placing foil over portions of baked goods *before* they start baking. Remove toward the end of baking time.

 When piping meringue onto a paper-lined tray, place a small dab of meringue at each corner of the tray before laying on the paper. Press the paper down at these spots, and the paper will not move on the tray.

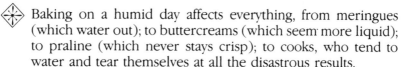 Baking on a humid day affects everything, from meringues (which water out); to buttercreams (which seem more liquid); to praline (which never stays crisp); to cooks, who tend to water and tear themselves at all the disastrous results.

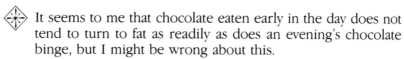 It seems to me that chocolate eaten early in the day does not tend to turn to fat as readily as does an evening's chocolate binge, but I might be wrong about this.

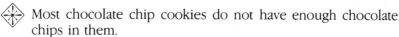 Most chocolate chip cookies do not have enough chocolate chips in them.

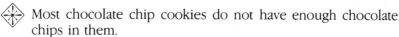 Always serve too much hot fudge sauce on hot fudge sundaes. It makes people overjoyed, and puts them in your debt.

Conversion Facts

*T*he following are conversion tables and other information for converting these recipes for use in other English-speaking countries. The cup and spoon measures given in this book are U.S. Customary; use these tables when working with British Imperial or metric kitchen utensils.

LIQUID MEASURES

*T*he old Imperial pint is larger than the U.S. pint; therefore note the following when measuring liquid ingredients.

U.S.	IMPERIAL
1 cup = 8 fluid ounces	1 cup = 10 fluid ounces
½ cup = 4 fluid ounces	½ cup = 5 fluid ounces
1 tablespoon = ¾ fluid ounce	1 tablespoon = 1 fluid ounce

U.S. MEASURE	METRIC	IMPERIAL*
1 quart	946 ml	1½+ pints
1 pint	473 ml	¾+ pint
1 cup	236 ml	−½ pint
1 tablespoon	15 ml	−1 tablespoon
1 teaspoon	5 ml	−1 teaspoon

*Note that exact quantities cannot always be given. Differences are more crucial when dealing with larger quantities. For teaspoon and tablespoon measures, simply use scant quantities, or for more accurate conversions rely upon metric measures.

WEIGHT AND VOLUME MEASURES

*U*nited States cooking procedures usually measure certain items by volume, although in the Metric or Imperial systems they are measured by weight. Here are some approximate equivalents for basic items appearing in this book.*

	U.S. CUSTOMARY	METRIC	IMPERIAL
Butter	1 cup	250 g	8 ounces
	½ cup	125 g	4 ounces
	¼ cup	62 g	2 ounces
	1 tablespoon	15 g	½ ounce
Cornstarch	1 teaspoon	10 g	⅓ ounce
Cream of Tartar	1 teaspoon	3–4 g	⅛ ounce
Flour (sifted all-purpose)	1 cup	128 g	4¼ ounces
	½ cup	60 g	2⅛ ounces
	¼ cup	32 g	1 ounce
Nut meats	1 cup	112 g	4 ounces
Raisins (or Sultanas)	¾ cup	125 g	4 ounces
Sugar: Granulated (Caster)	1 cup	240 g	8 ounces
	½ cup	120 g	4 ounces
	¼ cup	60 g	2 ounces
	1 tablespoon	15 g	½ ounce

	U.S. CUSTOMARY	METRIC	IMPERIAL
Confectioners'	1 cup	140 g	5 ounces
(Icing)	½ cup	70 g	3 ounces
	¼ cup	35 g	1+ ounce
	1 tablespoon	10 g	¼ ounce
Brown	1 cup	160 g	5⅓ ounces
	½ cup	80 g	2⅔ ounces
	¼ cup	40 g	1⅓ ounces
	1 tablespoon	10 g	⅓ ounce

*So as to avoid awkward measurements, some conversions are not exact.

OVEN TEMPERATURES

Gas Mark	¼	2	4	6	8
Fahrenheit	225	300	350	400	450
Centigrade	107	150	178	205	233

Recipes

sings Billie Holiday . . .

"I'd make a thousand trips

To his lips,

If I were a bee,

Because he's sweeter than

Chocolate candy to me . . . he's confectionary."

. . . all I can say is, he must have been *some* man.

Mousses, Puddings, Soufflés, and Other Desserts

*B*avarians, mousses, custards, and trifles fill this chapter: easy, chilled, do-ahead desserts that make entertaining a joy, particularly in warm weather.

For new inspirations try the handsome Bittersweet Chocolate Terrine, sure to amuse and delight guests and the single best dessert I know to serve a large crowd. Or prepare the quick and witty Chocolate Pâté, a thick, rich spread of glorious chocolate to be eaten with biscuits and fruit—another idea guaranteed to become a handy entertaining-set piece.

For cold weather, present guests or family with a comforting White Chocolate Gratin, with its crisp sugar crust. Or surprise them with a soufflé, hot and rippled, with dense, fudgey chocolate deep in its creamy interior.

Brandied Chocolate Bavarian

INGREDIENTS

3 tablespoons water
1½ envelopes unflavored gelatin
2 cups milk
3 ounces unsweetened chocolate
1 cup granulated sugar
6 egg yolks
1 teaspoon vanilla extract
1 tablespoon brandy or cognac, or to taste
2 cups heavy cream

*T*his is a basic bavarian recipe, followed by ideas for 2 spectacular presentations. The brandy flavoring enhances the rich chocolate essence of this creamy dessert.

1. Place water in a cup or small bowl. Sprinkle in the gelatin and set aside to soften.

2. Heat the milk with the chocolate in a saucepan until the chocolate has melted and the milk is just short of being scalded. Remove from heat.

3. Combine the sugar, egg yolks, and vanilla in a bowl. Beat with an electric hand mixer or whisk until exceedingly thick and pale, then slowly pour in the hot chocolate milk, beating all the while. Place the mixture in a saucepan over medium heat. Stirring constantly, let the mixture heat and thicken until, when you lift the spoon, a finger dragged down its back will leave a concise open track. Do not let the custard approach a boil.

4. Off the heat, add the softened gelatin to the custard and stir until it dissolves. Let the custard cool to warm, then add the cognac. Continue cooling (if you refrigerate the mixture, be sure to stir frequently and watch carefully), just until the bottom of the pan is at room temperature and custard is about to gel.

5. Rapidly whip the cream to a heavily thickened sludge that still moves but is not stiff. Fold the cream into the chocolate custard. Taste for brandy, and adjust flavoring if desired.

6. Splash some cold water into an 8-cup charlotte, soufflé, or ring mold. Shake out the excess, then pour in the bavarian. Let it chill until completely firm (at least 4 hours, although overnight improves flavor).

VARIATIONS

Chocolate Charlotte: Line an 8-cup charlotte mold with Chocolate Ladyfingers (page 114), then fill the center of the mold with the Brandied Chocolate Bavarian. Chill until firm, then decorate by sieving a bit of confectioners' sugar over the top and piping whipped cream rosettes around the base.

Chocolate Soufflé in a Chocolate Soufflé Dish: Make a Chocolate Soufflé Dish (page 174) using a 5- or 6-cup dish as a mold. Line the bottom of the chocolate dish with foil on the interior if you wish to reuse the dish and make a collar for the dish by folding over a length of heavy-duty foil, completely encircling the dish so that it stands 1½ inches above the rim of the dish. Tie a string around the foil to hold it in place, and lightly oil the inside rim of the collar. Pour a double recipe of the Brandied Chocolate Bavarian into the shell,

and chill until firm. Cut the string and remove the foil collar, then decorate the top with grated dark chocolate and rosettes of whipped cream.

3

White Chocolate Mousse

A very rich mousse that retains the delicate essence of white chocolate.

1. Melt the white chocolate over warm water. At the same time but in a separate pan, melt the butter.

2. Place white chocolate and butter in the bowl of an electric mixer (or you can beat the mixture with a hand-held mixer). Start beating the chocolate and butter together, and when they are mixed, add the egg yolks, 1 at a time. The mixture will separate and appear loose and splashy at first, but continue beating. After 5 minutes it will turn creamy and very thick. Stop the beating, but leave bowl on the mixer.

3. Beat the egg whites, preferably by hand. When they start to stiffen, sprinkle on the sugar a bit at

SERVES 8 TO 10

INGREDIENTS

12 ounces white chocolate, grated
1½ sticks unsalted butter
5 eggs, separated and at room temperature
½ cup granulated sugar

a time and continue beating until the egg whites form soft, glossy peaks.

4. Use the mixer on low speed to stir half of the egg whites into the chocolate. When they are just blended, fold in the remaining half of the whites by hand.

5. Spoon mixture into small individual dishes, pot de crème pots, or a large serving bowl. Cover and chill in the refrigerator. This mousse is better if allowed to sit overnight before it is served. It is delicious served plain with strong coffee, or place a scoop on a dessert plate and surround it with a thin lake of Nouvelle Chocolate Sauce (page 170).

Kit's Chocolate Mousse

A mousse with a rich, sophisticated texture and a flavor that hovers near heaven.

1. Melt the chocolate over hot water. Let it cool until only warm.

2. While the chocolate cools, whip the cream until it forms medium-stiff peaks. Do not overbeat or the mousse will lose some of its smooth, light texture.

3. Separate 4 of the eggs and set the whites aside. Combine yolks with the 2 remaining whole eggs in the bowl of an electric mixer. Beat until eggs are thick and lemon colored, around 5 minutes. While the yolks are beating, place the 4 egg whites in a clean copper or stainless-steel bowl and whisk, preferably by hand, until the whites start to stiffen. Sprinkle on the confectioners' sugar and beat until you have firm peaks.

SERVES 12 TO 15

INGREDIENTS

18 ounces semisweet chocolate
2 cups heavy cream, well chilled
6 eggs
2 tablespoons confectioners' sugar
2 tablespoons crème de cacao
1 tablespoon vanilla extract

4. Working quickly, add the cooled melted chocolate and a scoop of the whipped cream to the egg yolks. Stir until smooth, then add the remaining cream. When it is fully incorporated, add the liqueur and vanilla, then fold in the whites until just blended.

5. This mousse can be poured into small individual serving dishes or into 1 larger dessert dish. Chill at least 4 hours before serving. (Chilling it overnight intensifies the flavor.) The mousse may be frozen for up to 2 weeks. Remove from the freezer and let it sit in the refrigerator overnight before decorating.

VARIATION

Make the Brownie Cookie Crust (page 128), then fill it with Kit's Chocolate Mousse. Chill for 4 hours, then pipe whipped cream on top.

Chocolate Chestnut Mont Blanc

If you like chestnuts, combine them with chocolate in this variation on the classic French dessert. Mound the purée into a chocolate mountain, and top it with snowcaps of whipped cream and grated chocolate.

1. Place the sugar and water in a small saucepan. Clip on a candy thermometer. Over low heat, stir until the sugar has dissolved, then let the syrup simmer until it reaches 235 degrees.

2. At the same time, melt the chocolate over hot water. Place the chestnut purée and salt in the bowl of an electric mixer or a food processor and beat until smooth. Add the melted chocolate. As soon as the sugar syrup reaches the correct temperature, pour it slowly into the chestnut purée. Add the butter 1 tablespoon at a time. Scrape down the

SERVES 12 TO 15

INGREDIENTS

1 cup granulated sugar
¹/₃ cup water
1 cup semisweet chocolate chips
1 can (15¹/₂ ounces) chestnut purée
¹/₄ teaspoon salt
4 tablespoons unsalted butter, softened
Whipped cream, flavored with vanilla and sweetened to taste
1 ounce semisweet or bittersweet chocolate for grating
Glacéed chestnuts (optional)

sides of the bowl and make sure everything is well mixed.

3. Scrape the mixture into a small mixing bowl. Press a piece of plastic wrap directly over the top of the purée to keep it moist, then refrigerate until very chilled (overnight is fine).

4. To serve, turn out the purée onto a platter and form it into a mountain with a fork. Spoon or pipe a capping of whipped cream on the summit (or the mountain may be entirely masked in cream). Grate chocolate shavings on top and, if you wish, pipe rosettes of cream around the base. Garnish each rosette with a glacéed chestnut. This dessert is very rich, and I cannot eat much of the purée without diluting it with whipped cream.

Apricot Cream in a Chocolate Sack, page 46

Molded Chocolate Jelly

*H*ere is an old-fashioned choco-late jelly. With the addition of coffee, it becomes provocatively stim-ulating yet still suitable to serve to a maiden aunt.

1.   Soften the gelatin in ½ cup of the coffee.

2.   Place the water, salt, and chocolates in a saucepan and bring to a low boil, stirring all the while. When the chocolate has melted en-tirely, let the mixture simmer for 4 minutes. Stir it frequently.

3.   Remove chocolate from the heat and immediately add the gela-tin. Stir until the gelatin melts, then add the sugar and the remaining cof-fee. Stir until the sugar dissolves, then cool. When the mixture is at room temperature, add the vanilla.

4.   Pour chocolate mixture into a small mold and chill overnight in the refrigerator. To serve, dip the

SERVES 6 TO 8

INGREDIENTS

2 envelopes unflavored gelatin
1 cup strong coffee, cold
2 cups water
Pinch salt
1 ounce unsweetened chocolate
1 ounce semisweet chocolate
½ cup granulated sugar
1 teaspoon vanilla extract
Sweetened whipped cream

mold briefly into hot water, and turn out onto a glass serving plate. Sweet-ened whipped cream is a must with this dessert.

A Strawberry Tree with Bittersweet Chocolate Fondue, page 38

Chocolate Raspberry Trifle

This is a pretty sight layered in a clear glass bowl: the cocoa-colored ladyfingers, the dark red fruit, the stripes of custard piled mountain high with whipped cream—all topped with fudge sauce.

1.   To make the custard, bring the cream, 1½ cups of the milk, and the sugar just to a scald. Stir continuously so a skin will not form over the liquid. Remove from heat.

2.   Combine the remaining ½ cup of milk with the egg yolks. Slowly pour in the hot cream, stirring all the while. Place the mixture over medium-low heat and stir continuously until the custard thickens. Do not allow to approach a boil.

3.   Strain the custard through a sieve, then stir in the vanilla. Rub the lump of cold butter over the surface of the custard to form a protective

INGREDIENTS

*1 recipe Chocolate
   Ladyfingers (page 114)
   or slices of chocolate
   sponge or pound cake
Crème de cacao
White wine
1 recipe Hot Fudge Sauce
   (page 172), cooled, then
   thinned with water to a
   thick pouring consistency
1 quart fresh raspberries
2/3 cup heavy cream,
   whipped stiff and
   sweetened to taste
Sliced almonds, lightly
   toasted*

CUSTARD

*2 cups heavy cream
2 cups milk
2/3 cup granulated sugar
8 egg yolks
2 teaspoons vanilla extract
1 tablespoon unsalted
   butter, chilled*

barrier so the custard will not form a skin. Allow to cool. When the custard reaches room temperature, cover and refrigerate until chilled.

4.   Stir the butter into the custard before assembling the dessert.

5.   To build the trifle, arrange a dense layer of ladyfingers on the bottom of a large dessert bowl. Sprinkle them generously with crème de cacao and white wine. Drizzle on a third of the fudge sauce. Add half the custard.

6.   Arrange another layer of ladyfingers and sprinkle again with crème de cacao and white wine. Drizzle on another third of the sauce.

7.   Add slightly over half the berries in a layer. Top with remaining custard. If there is room in the dish, add another thin layer of ladyfingers sprinkled with liquor. Swirl

the whipped cream into a mountain on top of the custard. Arrange the remaining raspberries around the edge.

8. Put the whole dish in the refrigerator to chill. Just before serving, top the cream mountain with the sauce. Scatter on a handful of toasted almonds.

Chocolate and Vanilla Custard with Poached Pears

This is a pretty, slightly tart, 2-toned chocolate and vanilla custard. Its origins are Italian, as the ricotta indicates, and it makes a lovely summer dessert or an elegant ending to a large dinner party.

1. To prepare the pears, simmer the sugar and water together for 5 minutes. Add the vanilla. While sugar syrup is simmering, peel the pears, cut them in half, and remove the cores. Poach the pear halves immediately in sugar syrup to avoid discoloration. The pears should cook until just tender (10 to 15 minutes), but allow them to retain some firmness. Remove pears from the syrup. Pat dry and cut in very thin slices. Allow to cool.

2. Prepare the custard base. Heat the milk in a saucepan until scalded. Beat the egg yolks, sugar, and salt until thick and lemon col-

SERVES 10 TO 12

INGREDIENTS

1 cup granulated sugar
1½ cups water
1 teaspoon vanilla extract
2 firm medium pears
1 recipe Nouvelle Chocolate Sauce (page 170)

CUSTARDS

½ cup milk
4 eggs, separated
1¼ cups granulated sugar
Large pinch salt
2 envelopes unflavored gelatin, softened in ⅓ cup water
1 tablespoon lemon juice
4 ounces semisweet chocolate
1 pound cream cheese, at room temperature
8 ounces ricotta, at room temperature
2 to 3 tablespoons water
2 teaspoons vanilla extract
1 cup heavy cream

ored, then whisk the hot milk slowly into the eggs, pour mixture into a saucepan, and place pan on a gentle heat to thicken. Stir constantly, and do not allow to boil. When steam is rising from the custard, and just short of its breaking into a simmer, remove pan from the heat and stir in the softened gelatin. Stir until gelatin is totally dissolved, then add lemon juice. Strain custard through a sieve, and cool slightly, but do not let gel.

3. Melt the chocolate over hot water. Set aside.

4. In a large bowl, blend the cream cheese and ricotta with a fork or electric mixer. When the custard is cool, stir it into the cheese and mix thoroughly.

5. Move rapidly now. Divide the custard as equally as possible into 2 bowls. Add the chocolate to one half, the vanilla to the other.

6. Whip the cream until thick but not stiff, then divide the cream between the mixtures and blend into both.

7. Beat the egg whites to firm peaks, then fold half into each custard mixture.

8. Quickly run some cold water into a 10-inch springform pan and shake out the excess. Pour in the vanilla custard and smooth the top. Add the pear slices in a neat layer, then pour on the chocolate custard. Give the mold a gentle tap on a hard surface to settle the contents. Cover with plastic wrap and chill for at least 8 hours (overnight is even better).

9. Run a knife around the edge of the pudding, then turn the mold upside down on a serving platter. Soak a towel in hot water and wring out; place it on top of the custard mold. The custard will unmold shortly.

10. To serve, pour some of the Nouvelle Chocolate Sauce around the custard and serve the extra sauce in a sauceboat on the side.

Extra Bittersweet Chocolate Pots de Crème

Here is a rich, intensely chocolate dessert that is easily adaptable. If you do not care for orange flavoring, substitute ¹/₂ teaspoon instant coffee powder in the recipe. If you are a purist, add only a teaspoon of vanilla extract to the chocolate before it is poured into the serving dishes.

1. Preheat oven to 325 degrees. Place 8 pots de crème cups or small individual soufflé dishes in a baking pan.

2. Combine orange zest and sugar in a cup. With your fingers, rub the zest into the sugar to flavor it. Discard zest and set sugar aside.

3. Place cream in a saucepan. Stirring all the while, bring the cream to a scald over medium heat. Off the heat, add the chocolate, flavored sugar, and salt. Stir until the chocolate has completely melted.

SERVES 8

INGREDIENTS

1 inch length peeled orange zest
3 tablespoons granulated sugar
2 cups heavy cream
6 ounces bittersweet chocolate (preferably Tobler Extra-Bittersweet), chopped fine
Small pinch salt
5 egg yolks
1 tablespoon Grand Marnier

4. Place the egg yolks in a bowl and beat, preferably with an electric hand mixer, until thick. Slowly pour in half the hot chocolate mixture, beating all the while. Pour the egg mixture back into the saucepan and add remaining chocolate. Place pan over very low heat and stir constantly for 1 minute. Remove from the heat and add Grand Marnier.

5. Heat some water for the *bain-marie*.

6. Place a fine tea strainer over one of the molds and pour in some of the chocolate mixture. Continue filling molds, dividing mixture among the pots as evenly as possible. Cover the pots de crème, or place small saucers or a larger baking tray over the soufflé dishes. (This will keep the tops of the chocolate smooth, hole-free, and tender.)

7. Place a funnel at the side of the baking pan and pour the hot

water into the tin until it comes half way up the sides of the small dishes. Place pan in the oven and bake for 20 minutes.

8. Remove and uncover molds. Cool to room temperature, then re-cover the pots with tops or pieces of foil. Refrigerate. These are best served within 36 hours.

Steamed Fudge Pudding

A delicious moist, dense fudge pudding that could serve very well at the holiday season, especially if decorated with a cluster of candied cherry halves and 3 holly leaves.

1. Preheat oven to 350 degrees. Butter and sugar a 6-cup mold, preferably a charlotte, but a soufflé dish would also do. Arrange a *bain-marie* (a pan large enough to hold the baking mold surrounded by water). Set mold aside and fill the pan with 1 inch of water, then place in oven to heat.

2. Melt the chocolate over hot water. Set aside.

3. Put the egg yolks in the bowl of an electric mixer and beat until thick. Measure ¾ cup of sugar and gradually add it to the yolks, beating all the while. Beat until yolks become exceedingly thick and pale.

SERVES 12

INGREDIENTS

8 ounces semisweet chocolate, grated
6 eggs, separated and at room temperature
1 cup granulated sugar
2 tablespoons bread crumbs
1 teaspoon baking powder
2 teaspoons vanilla extract
⅓ cup mixed, chopped candied fruit (cherries, pineapple)
Generous ⅓ cup chopped dried figs
½ cup coarsely chopped pecans
½ cup red currant jelly (optional), heated until melted

4. Add the chocolate to the egg-yolk mixture and, with the mixer at a slow speed, add the bread crumbs, baking powder, vanilla, dried fruits, and nuts. The batter will be very stiff. Stop machine but leave bowl with beaters.

5. In a clean bowl, beat the egg whites until they start to stiffen. Continue beating and gradually add the remaining sugar. Beat until the whites hold soft glossy peaks.

6. Scoop half the whites into the pudding batter and let the machine mix them in at slow speed. Take the bowl from the mixer and fold the remaining whites into the batter as gently as possible.

7. Spoon batter into the prepared mold and cover the dish with a lid or foil. Place in *bain-marie* and bake for 2½ hours. (Add water if necessary to keep up the level.)

8. After baking, let the pudding cool to room temperature in the mold. When cool, turn the pudding out onto a platter. Cover with plastic wrap and chill. Serve slightly cool but not chilled.

9. For a slick, glazed look, the pudding can be brushed with melted red currant jelly. Or various dried and candied fruits can be arranged about the surface and the whole glossed with jelly glaze.

Chocolate Date-Nut Pudding

An old-fashioned classic, livened and enriched with the delicious crunch of chocolate chips.

1. Preheat oven to 350 degrees. Grease a 9 by 9-inch baking pan.

2. Place the dates in a sieve. Sprinkle over them 1 tablespoon of the flour, then mix with your fingers until all the pieces are coated. Shake the sieve to remove excess flour. Combine dates in a bowl with pecans and chocolate chips. Set aside.

3. Place egg yolks, sugar, and vanilla in a mixing bowl and beat until the eggs are thick and very light in color. Add the cream and continue beating for another minute.

4. In a separate bowl, beat the egg whites with salt until they form firm peaks.

5. Sprinkle remaining flour and the baking powder over the egg

SERVES 8 TO 10

INGREDIENTS

²⁄₃ cup pitted, chopped dates
2 tablespoons all-purpose flour
²⁄₃ cup coarsely chopped pecans
½ cup miniature semisweet chocolate chips
3 eggs, separated
²⁄₃ cup granulated sugar
½ teaspoon vanilla extract
¼ cup heavy cream
Pinch salt
1 teaspoon baking powder
Sweetened whipped cream, flavored with vanilla

yolks. Add the date-nut mixture, and stir gently together just until well blended. Stir in a third of the egg whites, then fold in the remaining whites. Pour mixture into baking pan and smooth surface. Bake for 35 minutes.

6. Remove pan from oven and let pudding cool completely before serving. Serve at room temperature with sweetened and flavored whipped cream.

Devil's Island

A dark, mysterious pudding that floats upon a secret syrup lake.

1. Preheat the oven to 350 degrees.

2. To make the syrup, heat the sugar and water in a small saucepan. Stir until it reaches a brisk simmer, then allow the syrup to cook for 15 minutes at a slow, frothing boil. Off the heat, add the rum.

3. While the syrup cooks, cream the sugar with the butter. Add the vanilla and set aside.

4. Sieve the dry ingredients together, then alternately fold the milk and the flour mixture into the butter mixture. Stir just until mixed, then fold in the nuts.

5. Pour the hot sugar syrup into an ungreased 6-cup soufflé dish or casserole. Drop the chocolate batter into syrup by tablespoonfuls.

SERVES 6 TO 8

INGREDIENTS

½ cup granulated sugar
3 tablespoons unsalted butter
1 teaspoon vanilla extract
1 teaspoon baking powder
4 tablespoons cocoa powder
1 cup all-purpose flour
½ teaspoon baking soda
½ cup milk
½ cup chopped pecans
Whipped cream

SYRUP

⅔ cup granulated sugar
2 cups water
1 tablespoon dark rum, or to taste

6. Bake for 45 to 50 minutes. The batter will expand to form a puffed surface, while the liquid turns itself into a rich, chocolate-rum sauce.

7. Serve hot or at room temperature with some unsweetened whipped cream.

White Chocolate Gratin

*H*ere is a pleasant pudding whose principal ingredient is white chocolate. It has a handsome golden gratin crust and tantalizing flavor. See if your guests can guess the main ingredient.

1. Prepare the topping by finely grating 2 ounces of the white chocolate. Cut the remaining ounce into slivers with a knife. (These should somewhat resemble slivered almonds.) Combine all the white chocolate with the cracker crumbs and set aside.

2. Preheat oven to 350 degrees. Butter a 10-inch gratin dish.

3. Melt the white chocolate for the filling over warm water.

4. Separate the eggs.

5. Place white chocolate and melted butter in the bowl of an electric mixer and begin to beat (never

SERVES 6 TO 7

INGREDIENTS

6 ounces white chocolate
3 eggs plus 1 egg white
5 tablespoons unsalted
 butter, melted
1 teaspoon vanilla extract
1 tablespoon crème de
 cacao
1/4 cup granulated sugar

TOPPING

3 ounces white chocolate
2 tablespoons coarse
 graham cracker crumbs

mind the odd consistency). Start adding the yolks, 1 at a time, to the chocolate, beating well after every addition. The mixture may separate and splash, but continue beating; all will become smooth. Add the vanilla and crème de cacao. Stop mixing, but keep the bowl on the machine.

6. In a separate bowl, beat the egg whites. When they start to thicken and firm, slowly add the sugar and continue beating to form stiff but not dry peaks.

7. Add a third of the whites to the white chocolate mixture and let the machine stir them in. Take the bowl off the machine and fold in the remaining whites by hand.

8. Spread the batter in the gratin dish and sprinkle the topping over the surface. Bake for 25 minutes, at which point a golden gratin will have formed over the surface. (Don't be alarmed at some col-

lapsing when the gratin comes from the oven.)

9. Serve at room temperature or just slightly cool (but not chilled) for best flavor. The gratin is best on the day it is made.

Bittersweet Chocolate Terrine

This chilled, neatly slicing dessert can be made in any 4-cup mold (a round soufflé or charlotte, for example), but it looks the most festive when shaped in a rectangular terrine. For a very large party, fill a traditional 8-cup, 11 by 4-inch terrine and double the recipe. Serve thin slices of this rich dessert with good, strong coffee.

1. Oil or butter a mold, preferably a rectangular terrine around 5 by 8 inches.

2. Peel the pistachio nuts by placing them briefly in boiling water. Turn off the heat and let them sit for 5 minutes, then rub briskly with a kitchen towel to remove the skins.

3. Mix together ⅓ cup of nuts, the raisins, the cherries, and the butter cookie bits. Set aside.

SERVES 12 TO 15

INGREDIENTS

⅔ cup shelled pistachio nuts
½ cup golden raisins, softened
½ cup red glacéed cherries, cut in half
1 package Pepperidge Farm Chessmen cookies, broken into ½-inch bits
6 ounces bittersweet chocolate
⅔ cup granulated sugar
4 tablespoons water
1 cup cocoa powder
1½ sticks unsalted butter, very soft
1 tablespoon Grand Marnier
1 egg plus 2 egg yolks, lightly beaten
Cocoa powder for garnishing

4. Melt the chocolate over warm water.

5. Place the sugar and water in a saucepan. Stir together over very low heat until the sugar is completely dissolved and the syrup is clear.

6. Place cocoa powder and softened butter in a bowl and stir together until they are smooth. Stir in the sugar syrup and then the melted chocolate and Grand Marnier. Add the eggs and mix well.

7. Gently fold in the dried fruit, nuts, and cookies, then immediately press the mixture into the prepared mold. Give the mold a good tap on a cloth-covered counter to ensure that the contents are settled. Cover and refrigerate at least overnight.

8. To unmold, run a knife around the sides of the terrine. Dip

the mold into a bowl of hot water, then invert onto a serving platter. (The terrine may need a good minute in and out of hot water to free itself. You can shake the mold and feel the chocolate move slightly when it is ready to turn out.) Let the terrine reharden completely in the refrigerator.

9. For serving, cut several slices of the terrine and let them overlap each other so that people can see the handsome mosaic of nuts and fruits. Sieve a bit of cocoa powder directly onto the top of the uncut terrine.

10. Chop the remaining pistachio nuts and border the cocoa-dusted top of the terrine. This dessert keeps well for a week.

Chocolate Pâté

*H*ere is an easy dessert suggestion. Arrange a platter of fresh fruits, particularly strawberries, pears, and whole, peeled navel oranges. Have another platter of excellent shortbread wedges, butter cookies, and semisweet English biscuits (like Carr's Whole Meal Biscuits). On a third platter, have 1 or 2 pretty cheeses and a crock of this smooth chocolate pâté.

1. In a small saucepan, melt the chocolates over hot water.

2. Place the cream in a saucepan and heat until scalded, stirring all the while. When the cream is just about to lift up into a boil, remove it from the heat. Add the melted chocolate and the butter, and stir briskly with a heavy spoon until the chocolate cools and thickens somewhat. Stir in the liqueur or extract and the chopped nuts.

SERVES 10 TO 12

INGREDIENTS

6 ounces semisweet chocolate

6 ounces bittersweet chocolate

1²/₃ cups heavy cream

5 tablespoons unsalted butter

2 teaspoons amaretto, or ¹/₄ teaspoon almond extract

1¹/₄ cups chopped (medium fine) blanched almonds, toasted

3. Spoon the chocolate mixture into a small pâté or cheese crock and smooth the surface. Press plastic wrap directly down onto the surface of the chocolate to keep it from hardening.

4. If the pâté is to be served within 2 or 3 hours, leave at room temperature. If it is to be served in a day or two, refrigerate the mixture, but then it may be necessary to add a bit of warm cream to the chocolate to soften and smooth the consistency, even after the pâté has been brought to room temperature.

5. Stick a small butter knife in the crock before serving.

Chocolate Baumkuchen, page 72

Chocolate Parfait

A delicious cold dessert that should be eaten just short of frozen. Its texture is very suave.

1. Place the milk in a pan and heat over a double boiler until hot. Add the chocolate and stir until the chocolate melts. Add the sugar, then continue stirring in the double boiler until the mixture is smooth.

2. Place a tray's worth of ice cubes in a large bowl. Set the pan containing the chocolate mixture over the ice and stir until the bottom of the pan is no longer hot.

3. Start beating the mixture with an electric hand mixer. Slowly add the cream until the chocolate mixture is very smooth. Continue adding the rest of the cream more rapidly, and beat until the whole is the consistency of lightly whipped cream. It is most important to stop whipping before the cream thickens

SERVES 15

INGREDIENTS

¹/₂ cup milk
5 ounces unsweetened chocolate
1¹/₃ cups granulated sugar
4 cups heavy cream
2 teaspoons vanilla extract
Grated semisweet chocolate or chopped pecans (optional)

too much, as overbeating will keep the parfait from having the lovely, light yet rich texture that you want.

4. Put the chocolate cream into a glass or stainless-steel mixing bowl. Cover with plastic wrap and put into the freezer. Four hours after the parfait has started freezing, take it out and beat it briefly with a hand mixer so that any hardening portions at the edges are dispersed. Replace in freezer until ready to serve.

5. I like best to eat this on the day it is made and after it has been frozen from 6 to 8 hours. Heap it into parfait glasses, and top with grated chocolate or chopped pecans if you like.

Chocolate Raspberry Torte, page 64

Chocolate Omelet

This is a fluffy chocolate omelet which encases a scoop or two of ice cream.

1. Have everything premeasured and ready. Place a 9-inch frying or omelet pan on stove and add butter; have it ready to heat. Flatten the ice cream scoops into 2 ovals each 5 inches long. Sandwich together and place in the freezer. Push the confectioners' sugar through a small sieve. Have a small platter ready for the omelet. Preheat the broiler.

2. Place egg yolks and 2 tablespoons of granulated sugar in the bowl of an electric mixer or in a food processor fitted with a plastic blade. Beat at a high speed.

3. Meanwhile, start whisking the egg whites by hand. When they are beginning to firm, sprinkle the remaining granulated sugar, 1

SERVES 2

INGREDIENTS

1 tablespoon unsalted
 butter
2 large scoops vanilla ice
 cream
1 tablespoon confectioners'
 sugar
2 large eggs, separated and
 at room temperature
4 tablespoons granulated
 sugar
Pinch ground cinnamon
1 heaping tablespoon
 cocoa powder

spoonful at a time, onto the whites and continue beating until they form firm but glossy peaks.

4. Start butter melting in pan.

5. By hand, gently stir the cinnamon, cocoa powder, and a large scoop of the egg whites into the egg yolks. Fold in the remaining whites gently but rapidly.

6. Take the ice cream from the freezer and keep it near the stove.

7. When the butter has foamed and subsided, scrape in the omelet mixture and smooth it over. Cook over medium heat until the bottom of the omelet has firmed in the pan and begun to firm around the sides. Quickly transfer the omelet to under the broiler and let the top just begin to firm (the insides will remain hot but unset).

8.   Remove omelet from broiler and place the ice cream on half. Gently lift the other half up and over the ice cream, then slide the omelet out of the pan and onto a platter.

9.   Immediately sift the confectioners' sugar over the surface and eat at once. The sugared top of the omelet will be just slightly crisp; the ice cream and loose eggy chocolate on the interior will melt into a delicious half-sauce.

Mandarin Chocolate Omelet Soufflé

INGREDIENTS

*¾ cup granulated sugar,
  approximately*
*3 ounces semisweet
  chocolate*
*Zest from ½ orange,
  minced very fine*
2 teaspoons Grand Marnier
*6 eggs plus 3 egg whites, at
  room temperature*

*H*ere is a light chocolate version
of a classic soufflé omelet. The
thin, sugary crusts on top and bottom play nicely against the creamy,
mellow fluff of the interior. I use this
recipe infrequently, but sometimes it
is the perfect answer to a last-minute
dilemma when a sudden, large
number of guests appear under the
most casual of circumstances. Hand
everyone a spoon and let each dig
into the frothy mixture. Note: the egg
whites must be whipped by hand.

1. Organization is essential to
this recipe; have all your equipment
and ingredients prepared ahead.
Preheat oven to as high as it will
go.

2. Butter a stainless-steel serving tray, quiche dish, or gratin at
least 12 inches long. Strew ¼ cup of
sugar on the bottom of the dish and
shake the dish to distribute sugar
evenly. Place the dish in freezer. If

you are going to whisk the egg
whites in a copper bowl, clean it
impeccably. Fit a large pastry bag
with a rosette tube.

3. Melt the chocolate over hot
water. Set aside.

4. Combine remaining sugar,
orange zest, and Grand Marnier in a
small bowl. Rub the mixture between your fingers to impregnate
the sugar with orange essence.

5. Separate the eggs. Place
yolks and orange sugar in the bowl
of an electric mixer and start beating
at medium speed. Continue beating
while you prepare egg whites.

6. Beat the egg whites until
they form firm peaks.

7. Fold the melted chocolate
into the very thick yolk mixture.
Fold the whites into the yolks. Work
rapidly and never mind if everything
is not completely mixed; the impor-

tant thing is to keep a stiff egg-white volume.

8. Scoop a third of the eggs into the pastry bag. Remove sugared dish from freezer and scrape out the remaining eggs in a domed oval onto the cold dish. Quickly pipe a rough design on the mix with the pastry bag: fat rosettes in a row over the top center, squiggles around the base of the omelet.

9. Sprinkle omelet with a huge handful of sugar and pop omelet into the hot oven. In about 1 to 2 minutes, the soufflé should be lightly browned on the top. Remove from oven and eat at once.

Chocolate Ripple Soufflé

A vanilla-based soufflé patterned with rich veins of chocolate.

1. Preheat oven to 400 degrees. Butter and sugar a 6- or 7-cup soufflé dish, then set dish in a cool spot.

2. Melt the chocolate over hot water. Set aside.

3. In a heavy saucepan, combine the sugar, flour, and ¼ teaspoon of salt. Slowly stir in the cold milk. Bring to a boil over medium heat, stirring constantly. Regulate heat to a simmer, then continuously stir the custard base until it is the consistency of a thick white sauce. Off the heat, add the butter and stir until it dissolves.

4. Separate the eggs. To the 5 yolks, add a large spoonful of the custard base and stir well; then add the warmed yolks to the custard. Re-

SERVES 6

INGREDIENTS

2 ounces semisweet chocolate
⅓ cup granulated sugar
2 tablespoons all-purpose flour
Salt
1 cup cold milk
1 tablespoon unsalted butter
5 eggs plus 2 egg whites
1½ tablespoons vanilla extract
1 teaspoon kirsch (optional)

serve ¼ cup of the custard mixture and set aside.

5. To the remaining custard, add the vanilla and the kirsch. (The optional kirsch will intensify the flavoring though not reveal its own character.)

6. Stir the reserved ¼ cup of custard into the melted chocolate.

7. Beat the egg whites with a pinch of salt until they form firm, glossy peaks. (Preferably this should be done by hand in a clean copper bowl.) Fold two thirds of the whites into the vanilla mixture. Fold the remaining third into the chocolate.

8. Put the vanilla custard into the prepared soufflé dish. Pour on the chocolate mixture and gently, briefly, turn and fold it into the vanilla base so that it forms large, striking swirls. Do not overwork.

9. Place soufflé immediately into the hot oven and bake for 20 minutes. Sprinkle a large handful of sugar over the top and continue baking for 5 additional minutes (for a semi-custard in the center) or 10 minutes (for a firm soufflé). Serve at once.

Spiced Chocolate Pudding

This is a gentle soufflé that rises then falls into a dense, flavorful pudding.

1. Preheat oven to 350 degrees. Pour water into a large cake pan or roasting pan until it is 1 inch deep, then place on the middle rack of the oven; this is your *bain-marie*.

2. Generously butter an 8-cup soufflé dish. Spoon a scoop of granulated sugar into the dish and rotate the dish until the sugar adheres generously to the bottom and sides. Refrigerate until needed.

3. Cream the butter and sugar together. Stir in the flour, instant coffee, and spices, and mix until smooth. Set aside.

4. Place milk and chocolate in a medium-sized saucepan. Stir over low heat until the chocolate melts and the milk begins to simmer

SERVES 8 TO 10

INGREDIENTS

1 stick unsalted butter, softened
2/3 cup granulated sugar
2/3 cup all-purpose flour
1/2 teaspoon instant coffee powder
1/4 teaspoon powdered cinnamon
1/4 teaspoon powdered allspice
1/4 teaspoon ground ginger
Pinch grated nutmeg
2/3 cup milk
2 ounces semisweet chocolate
2 ounces unsweetened chocolate
5 eggs, separated
1 1/2 cups heavy cream

TOPPING

Vanilla extract
Powdered cinnamon
Granulated sugar

around the edges. Slowly whisk the milk into the flour mixture, then return entire mixture to the saucepan.

5. Place the pudding base over medium heat. Stir constantly with a wooden spoon as the mixture heats and thickens. Keep stirring vigorously until the batter comes away from the sides of the pan and begins to dry somewhat on the bottom of the dish. Remove from heat.

6. Whisk the egg whites until they form firm peaks.

7. Stir the egg yolks and then a third of the whites into the chocolate mixture. Fold the remaining whites gently into the mixture until just incorporated, but do not overwork.

8. Quickly scrape the chocolate mixture into the prepared soufflé dish. Smooth the surface lightly, and place the dish in the *bain-marie*.

9.   Bake for 35 to 40 minutes. Remove from oven, let stand for 5 minutes, then run a knife around the edge of the pudding. Place a platter over the top of the dish and reverse the pudding onto it.

10.   Whip heavy cream until slightly thickened but still pourable. Flavor with vanilla, a pinch of cinnamon, and sugar to taste. (I like the grainy feeling of the undissolved sugar in this cream.) Serve the pudding hot or warm, with a pitcher of cream on the side.

Frozen Mexican Chocolate

SERVES 12

INGREDIENTS

8 ounces semisweet
  chocolate
8 ounces bittersweet
  chocolate
6 egg yolks
1 tablespoon vanilla-
  extract
1/2 teaspoon powdered
  cinnamon
2 cups heavy cream, cold
Whipped cream for garnish

*T*he combination of vanilla and cinnamon in Hot Mexican Chocolate (page 160) is so endearing that, to honor the components, I had to create another dessert at the opposite extreme of the temperature scale.

It is most important that the cream, in both its initial and final whippings, not be overworked. Stop short rather than tightening the cream and risking a dry consistency.

1. To prepare the mold, lightly oil a 9-inch square or round baking pan. Line the pan with aluminum foil and also give the foil a light oiling.

2. Melt the chocolate over warm water. Remove from heat when it is soft.

3. Place the egg yolks in a bowl and whisk them by hand until they are thick and light. Stir in the vanilla and cinnamon.

4. Immediately place the cream in the bowl of an electric mixer and beat just until it thickens. (It should not hold a peaked form.) Scrape the egg yolks into the cream and mix briefly.

5. Start stirring the chocolate with a wooden spoon until the chocolate is glossy and no longer warm. With the mixer on low speed, add the cooled chocolate to the eggs and cream and beat just until the chocolate is totally integrated. Immediately pour the mixture, which should be the consistency of lightly whipped cream, into the prepared mold. Cover mold with foil, then place in the freezer overnight.

6. To unmold, run a knife between the inside of the pan edges and the foil. Tear off portions of edg-

ing foil so that the foil becomes even with the filling, then reverse the dessert onto a serving platter. Rub a hot sponge over the pan bottom, and the dessert should slide out.

7.   Peel off the foil. Let the dessert mellow for 30 minutes at room temperature before serving, then pipe rosettes of whipped cream around the edge of the dessert for a garnish.

Fruits and Fantasies

*F*or every lover of chocolate who is a romantic at heart, this chapter celebrates the sensuous hearts and flowers of chocolate. Herein sprout strawberry trees with not 1 but 2 delectable fondues for dipping; pears with thimblefuls of fragrant liquor hidden at their core and circlings of bittersweet chocolate lace; nests of chocolate candy holding truffle eggs; and 2 imaginative chocolate-covered creams, one a chocolate sack spilling over with apricot cream and raspberries, the other a pale pink pudding twined with chocolate ivy and delicately flavored with roses.

Fruit Curry with Chocolate and Condiments

This easy and unusual dessert (or whole luncheon for that matter) can be composed at table. Portions could be large or small, so the following recipe is basically a procedural guide. Make the condiment bowl of grated chocolate particularly generous. Chocolate lovers will adore spooning on quantities of bittersweet flakes, and the richly aromatic sauce that results when the chocolate melts into the warm spiced fruit is delicious.

1. Have the condiments arranged on a tray. Pile the cookies in a small basket.

2. Peel and cut the fruits (except the banana and passion fruit) into large, bite-sized pieces. Place anything that might discolor in a bowl of water with lemon water.

SERVES 4

INGREDIENTS

5 or 6 varied fruits:
   Pineapple
   Mango, papaya, or peach
   Pear, apple, or banana
   Kiwi
   Strawberries or cherries
   Passion fruit if possible,
      and any other exotic
      fruit available except
      the citrus family
Lemon juice

CURRY SAUCE

2 tablespoons unsalted
   butter
1 tablespoon granulated
   sugar
1 tablespoon brown sugar
1 tablespoon lemon juice
1/4 teaspoon powdered
   cinnamon
1/2 teaspoon ground ginger
Scrapings of nutmeg
3 tablespoons dark rum

3. To make the curry sauce, place the butter, sugars, lemon juice, and spices in a 10-inch skillet. Place skillet over high heat and melt the butter and sugar, stirring all the time. Add the rum and any firm fruits (pears, pineapple, peach-colored fruits). Let the fruit sauté briefly as the syrup turns thick and glossy.

4. Peel the banana. Off the heat, add the remaining fruits including the banana, and shake the pan to warm them. If you are using passion fruit, scoop out its seeds and juice and add at this time. Serve the warm fruits at once.

NOTE

For an elegant presentation, center a brass tray or lazy Susan holding all the condiments on the table. Place a vase of jasmine or other exotic blossoms among them.

For those fond of pyrotechnics, it is possible to prepare the sugar and butter glaze, add all the fruit, then pour on rum which has been warmed and flame the whole dish. Shake the pan until the flames go out, then serve at once.

CONDIMENTS

A bowl of each of:
  *Grated bittersweet
    chocolate*
  *Lightly toasted sliced
    almonds*
  *Toasted shredded
    coconut*
  *Currants or golden
    raisins*
  Candied mint leaves
  *Chopped crystallized
    ginger*
*Giant Crisp Chocolate
  Wafers (page 122)*

A Strawberry Tree with Two Fondues

*C*ocoa Balls (page 123) would also be amusing to dip into these luscious mixtures.

1. To make the tree, cover the Styrofoam cone with the moss. Wrap the wire around the moss and push the ends of the wire into the foam to hold on the moss.

2. Stick a toothpick into the end of each strawberry and insert the picks in rows around the tree. (The green moss should show between each strawberry row). Insert among the greenery if you wish, a few leaves or flowers. Place the tree on a pedestal or cake stand.

3. To make the white fondue, melt the white chocolate with ½ cup of evaporated milk over very low heat. Off the heat, add the vanilla and more evaporated milk as necessary to bring the chocolate to a coating consistency.

SERVES 12 TO 15

INGREDIENTS

2 quarts large strawberries, washed and hulled
Ivy or galax leaves
Flower buds (optional)

WHITE FONDUE

12 ounces white chocolate, grated
⅔ cup evaporated milk
¼ teaspoon vanilla extract

BITTERSWEET FONDUE

6 ounces bittersweet chocolate, grated
6 ounces semisweet chocolate, grated
¾ cup heavy cream
Flavoring of choice: Grand Marnier, cognac, etc.

TREE

1 Styrofoam cone, about 12 to 15 inches high
Florist's moss
Green florist's wire

4. To make the chocolate fondue, melt the dark chocolates with the cream. Off the heat, add the flavoring of your choice.

5. Pour the fondues into warmed fondue pots or chafing dishes on either side of the strawberry tree. Guests pluck off the berries and dip them into the chocolates.

38

Almond Roca Cake, page 66

Chocolate-Dipped Pineapple with Melba Sauce

This combination of ripe pineapple with bittersweet chocolate is most refreshing. And it is a dessert that is so simple, so elegant.

1. Cut off the pineapple's leafy top. With a large knife, slice the skin off the pineapple in long, downward strips. (Cut off enough so that the eyes are removed in the process.)

2. Cut the pineapple into round slices ½ to ¾ inch thick. Cut each slice into 3 or 4 sections, and cut the inedible core from each portion to form large, triangular wedges. Place wedges on a platter.

3. Sprinkle the pineapple with some rum and 2 tablespoons of sugar, and chill for at least 1 hour before serving.

4. Prepare the melba sauce. Purée and sieve the berries to remove seeds from frozen raspberries. Sweeten to taste with sugar, and add

SERVES 6 TO 8

INGREDIENTS

1 ripe pineapple
Light rum
Granulated sugar
2 packages frozen
* raspberries, or 1 quart*
* fresh raspberries*
6 ounces bittersweet
* chocolate (preferably*
* Tobler Extra-bittersweet),*
* chopped*

a touch of rum to taste. Chill until needed.

5. Melt the chocolate over warm water.

6. To assemble the dessert, remove the pineapple from the refrigerator and blot wedges dry. Cover a baking sheet with wax paper. Dip the narrow half of each wedge into the chocolate until the portion is half coated. Place dipped sections on the cookie sheet and let them harden briefly in refrigerator.

7. Pour a thin pool of raspberry purée into the center of each individual dessert plate. Arrange 2 or 3 wedges of pineapple on top of the sauce just before serving.

Chocolate Strawberry Shortcake, page 76

Chocolate Crêpes with Fresh Cherry Filling

Ripe cherries with the crunch of bittersweet chocolate bits form the filling for chocolate crêpes.

1. Wash and pit the cherries. Place them in a bowl and run a knife through them to chop them coarsely. (Chop them in the bowl so as not to lose precious juices.)

2. Stir in the vanilla, kirsch, cinnamon, lemon juice, and sugar, and let the cherries sit for 1 hour so they can become a juicy filling.

3. To make the crêpes, sift the cocoa, flour, salt, and sugar into a mixing bowl. Make a well in the middle and add the eggs, milk, vanilla, and melted butter. The batter should be the consistency of heavy cream; add more milk if necessary.

4. Heat a seasoned crêpe pan or a lightly buttered frying pan. (The pan should be hot enough so that a drop of batter sizzles when it is test-

SERVES 8
INGREDIENTS

1 pound ripe bing cherries
1 teaspoon vanilla extract
2 tablespoons kirsch
Pinch ground cinnamon
1 tablespoon lemon juice
¼ cup granulated sugar
3 ounces bittersweet chocolate, cut into bits
Vanilla ice cream or sweetened whipped cream
Cocoa powder for dusting

CRÊPES

2 tablespoons cocoa powder, preferably Dutch process
⅓ cup all-purpose flour
Pinch salt
2 tablespoons granulated sugar
2 eggs
¾ cup milk, plus additional for thinning
1 teaspoon vanilla extract
3 tablespoons unsalted butter, melted

ed.) Add a ladle of batter to the hot pan, quickly roll and turn the pan to spread the batter, then pour excess batter back into bowl. Cook until brown speckles appear on top of the pancake, then turn it over briefly to cook on the other side.

5. When ready to serve, assemble the crêpes. Stir chocolate bits into cherry filling. Place a large spoon of filling down the center of a crêpe, and roll up the crêpe. Place on individual plate. Continue to fill and roll crêpes; serve 2 crêpes to a plate.

6. Top each serving with a small scoop of vanilla ice cream or a large dollop of thick whipped cream. Place a small amount of cocoa in a sieve and quickly dust the top of each serving.

Crisp Banana Fritters with Fudge Sauce

A good, warming winter dessert—
a fudge sundae in reverse.

1. One hour before the fritters are to be made, prepare both bananas and fritter batter. Peel the bananas, cut into ¾-inch slices, and place in a bowl. Sprinkle immediately with lemon juice, a generous dash of liquor, and the sugar. Toss slices gently so that all are coated, then leave to steep for 1 hour. Blot dry before dipping in batter.

2. To prepare the batter, place the flour, salt, and sugar in a bowl and stir together. Make a well in the center and add the egg yolk, beer, milk, and melted butter. Gently stir the liquid into the flour, mixing only until perfectly blended. Place a towel over the bowl and leave in a warm place for 1 hour.

3. Just before needed, heat the frying oil in a deep sauté pan or oth-

SERVES 8

INGREDIENTS

3 large bananas
Juice of 1 lemon
Rum or Grand Marnier
2 tablespoons granulated
  sugar
Peanut or vegetable oil for
  frying
Granulated sugar
Hot Fudge Sauce (page
  172), cooled and diluted
  with heavy cream to a
  thick pouring consistency

BATTER

¾ cup all-purpose flour
Pinch salt
1 teaspoon granulated
  sugar
1 egg, separated
⅓ cup warm beer
1 to 2 teaspoons milk
2 tablespoons unsalted
  butter, melted

er frying unit. Whisk the egg white to soft peaks and fold it into the batter. When a drop of batter immediately sizzles and bobs, the oil is ready for frying.

4. Dip a few pieces of banana at a time into the batter, then fry them to golden puffs. Do not overcrowd them in the pan.

5. Drain fritters on paper toweling, then roll them in extra granulated sugar. When all are fried, place portions on dessert plates, pour on the fudge sauce, and serve at once.

Rose Pudding Twined with Chocolate Ivy

This is to be made in summer, when rose petals are plentiful. Here is a pale pink cream unmolded and twined about with chocolate stems and ivy leaves; it is a dessert that is ravishing served with a compote of raspberries or strawberries on the side, a dessert that will remind you of a perfumed chocolate-covered cream.

1. To make a rose syrup, combine the sugar and water in a medium saucepan. Bring to a boil, then regulate the heat to a simmer and cook for 5 minutes. Add the rose petals, simmer another 3 minutes, then remove pan from the heat and add the lemon juice and softened gelatin. Stir until the gelatin dissolves, then cover the pan and allow to infuse until the syrup reaches room temperature.

2. Strain the rose syrup through a fine sieve, pressing down

INGREDIENTS

1 cup granulated sugar
2³/₄ cups water
Clean, dry rose petals from 20 red and/or pink roses
1¹/₂ teaspoons lemon juice
2¹/₂ envelopes gelatin, softened in ¹/₄ cup cold water
Red and yellow food coloring
1 teaspoon rose water (available at specialty food shops)
2 cups heavy cream, chilled

IVY

4 ounces semisweet or bittersweet chocolate
7 ivy leaves of varying sizes
2 or 3 small pink or peach-colored roses

on the rose petals in the process to extract all possible essence. Add 5 drops of red food coloring and 2 drops of yellow to the syrup. Stir in rose water.

3. Place the syrup in the refrigerator and stir frequently as it cools. Just as the syrup threatens to set, whip the cream until lightly thickened. Add in the rose syrup and continue beating at low speed just until the cream is uniformly pink.

4. Lightly oil an 8-cup charlotte mold, a round metal bowl, or a 10-inch cake pan. Pour in the rose cream. Cover and refrigerate at least 2 hours before eating.

5. Melt the chocolate for the ivy over hot water.

6. To make the ivy, use a pastry brush to coat the *back* side of the ivy leaves with the melted chocolate. Wipe off any chocolate from the

front side of the leaves. Place on a tray and let harden in the refrigerator for 5 minutes. Peel leaves off the chocolate, starting with stem end.

7. To assemble, dip the pudding mold briefly in hot water, then unmold onto a serving dish. Remelt the remaining chocolate and spoon it into a pastry bag fitted with a ¼-inch-wide plain tube (or into a paper bag; see page xviii). Pipe 2 heavy strands of intertwining ivy stem around the surface of the rose pudding, staying mainly around the rim. Place the chocolate leaves at random around the stems, then place the pudding in the refrigerator to harden the chocolate in place.

8. Just before serving, add 2 or 3 fresh roses to the assemblage.

Pears with Bittersweet Chocolate Lace

The classic Poires Hélène recipe calls for poached pears on a bed of vanilla ice cream, with hot chocolate sauce and crystallized violets as garnish. Here is a lightened variation on the theme, with crème anglaise substituting for the ice cream and chocolate lace instead of sauce.

1. To make the poaching syrup, bring the water, sugar, and cinnamon to a boil, then reduce heat and simmer for 5 minutes. Set aside until needed.

2. To make the crème anglaise, place milk in a saucepan. Bring to a scald, stirring all the time. Remove from heat.

3. Whisk the sugar and egg yolks together until thick and creamy. Slowly stir in the hot milk, then return to saucepan and place custard on low heat and stir con-

SERVES 4

INGREDIENTS

4 large firm pears,
 preferably with stems
1 lemon, quartered
4 ounces bittersweet
 chocolate
Pear brandy, or light rum
 or other liquor of choice
Fresh violet flowers, or 4
 small green leaves

POACHING SYRUP

3½ cups water
2 cups granulated sugar
1 stick cinnamon
2 teaspoons vanilla extract

CRÈME ANGLAISE

1 cup milk
3 tablespoons granulated
 sugar
3 egg yolks
1 teaspoon vanilla extract

stantly until it thickens to a sauce of medium consistency. Do not allow to simmer.

4. Strain the sauce through a sieve, then allow to cool. When it is cool, stir in the vanilla. Cover and refrigerate until needed.

5. Place the poaching syrup back on the heat, add the vanilla, and bring to a simmer.

6. Peel the pears neatly (do not core them), and immediately rub the fruit with a lemon section to preserve whiteness. Poach the pears, covered, until they are just tender. Remove pears from syrup and let drain and cool.

7. With an apple corer, cut straight down over the stem and out through the end of the pears. Cut a half-inch from each end of the cores and insert piece in the bottom of each pear to plug it. Cut off a half-

inch at the stem end of the cores and reserve the pieces.

8. Melt the chocolate over warm water. Line a cookie sheet with wax paper.

9. Place the melted chocolate into a pastry bag fitted with a small script writing tip, or into a paper piping bag (page xviii). Pipe a bit of chocolate into each pear to seal the plugged ends. Refrigerate pears.

10. Pipe out the remaining chocolate into a small lacy pattern on the wax paper. Place cookie sheet in refrigerator to firm chocolate.

11. The pears may be assembled and served individually or on 1 large platter. Place pear on an individual dessert plate or all the pears on a serving platter. Spoon crème anglaise around (sauce should not be too cold). Spoon into the hollow

of the pears a small thimbleful of liquor, then replace stem plugs.

12. Break off small portions of chocolate lace and place them around the edge of the floating sauce. Scatter 3 or 4 violet flowers over each pear (they are edible). Failing violets, sprout a green leaf from each stem.

Apricot Cream in a Chocolate Sack

SERVES 10

INGREDIENTS

1 cup granulated sugar
2 cups water
1 cup dried apricots
2 envelopes gelatin,
*   softened in 1/4 cup water*
1 tablespoon lemon juice
1 1/2 cups heavy cream

MELBA SAUCE

2 pints fresh raspberries, or
*   2 packages frozen*
*   raspberries*
Granulated sugar as
*   needed*

SACK

12 ounces semisweet,
*   couverture, or*
*   compound chocolate*
Small #6 paper bag (6 by
*   4 by 11 inches)*
Fresh apricots, raspberries,
*   strawberries (any or all),*
*   and a handful of flowers*

*H*ere is one of the handsomest and most amusing presentations I know. Coat a paper bag with chocolate and let it harden. Peel away the paper and fill the chocolate bag with apricot bavarian, then add berries and a spill of fruit around the bag and present the whole display as an elegant dessert.

1. To make the apricot cream, combine the sugar and water in a saucepan. Bring to a boil and then regulate to a simmer. Let the syrup cook 5 minutes. Add the apricots to the saucepan and let them simmer until completely tender. Stir the apricots frequently and don't let them scorch.

2. Off the heat, add the gelatin and stir until it is dissolved. Purée the apricots in a food processor or press them through a sieve. There should be 2½ cups of purée; add a bit of water if necessary to make this measurement. Stir in lemon juice.

3. Let the apricot mixture cool in the refrigerator briefly. Stir the purée frequently, and just as it begins to set, whip the cream until lightly thickened and fold it into the apricots.

4. Sprinkle a metal or glass loaf pan (about 9 by 5 inches) with a few drops of cold water and shake out the excess. Pour apricot cream into pan and refrigerate until set.

5. To make the sauce, press the fresh or frozen berries through a sieve and add sugar to taste. The sauce should not be overly sweet. Place in a pitcher and refrigerate until needed.

6. Melt the chocolate over hot water. Set aside.

7. To make the sack, first cut off an even 2 inches around the top of the paper bag, preferably with pinking shears. Cut a small, rounded indention like that found on the

front side of most paper sacks. Coat the exterior of the sack thoroughly with vegetable oil, then rub off any excess oil with paper toweling. Stack 1 or 2 large cans upright on a tray. Open the sack and insert the sack over the top. (The paper bag should now have all sides and surfaces free and not touching the tray.)

8. Using a pastry brush, coat the sack with a very thick layer of melted chocolate. Especially reinforce the creases at sides and bottom. Place the tray holding the sack in the refrigerator to harden the chocolate. When hardened, take out and repeat coating process then harden again.

9. To assemble, carefully peel the paper bag away from the chocolate and work it out. (If a side should separate, it can be cemented together with a bit of melted chocolate.) Spoon the apricot cream into the bag. The bag can either stand up-

right, with berries on top of the cream and more fruit at the foot of the bag, or the whole sack can be placed on its side on a platter, as if it had tipped over and was spilling its contents. Strew berries, apricots, and a handful of flowers out from the top of the sack in a large spill.

10. Place the platter on the table and serve the sauce in its pitcher on the side. To serve, simply crack into the sack with a spoon and serve luscious portions of apricot cream topped with a wedge of chocolate.

Pink Pears on a Chocolate Tart

A pretty fantasy for a midsummer's night: pear halves poached pink in a raspberry syrup, placed on a crisp, chocolate-glazed crust. This tart should be made and composed shortly before eating, though the pears can be poached ahead.

1. Prepare a syrup in which to poach the pears. Combine the sugar, water, and raspberry purée in a saucepan. Bring to a simmer and cook 5 minutes.

2. Peel, core, and halve the pears. Rub them immediately with the lemon juice to preserve their whiteness.

3. Add the vanilla to the syrup and poach the pears just until they are tender. Remove pears and drain them well. Place pears on a layer of paper toweling and cover with plastic wrap. Chill until needed.

SERVES 10 TO 12
INGREDIENTS
1 cup granulated sugar
2½ cups water
1 cup strained raspberry purée, made from fresh or frozen berries
6 to 7 firm large pears
Juice of 1 lemon
1 teaspoon vanilla extract
4 ounces semisweet chocolate
3 tablespoons raspberry jam, warmed
2 tablespoons red currant jelly, melted
Mint leaves
Crystallized roses, preferably whole

CRUST
¼ cup ground hazelnuts
½ cup ground almonds
1 tablespoon cornstarch
Pinch ground cinnamon
½ cup granulated sugar
4 egg whites, at room temperature

4. To prepare the crust, preheat oven to 375 degrees. Grease and flour a large baking sheet and trace a 12-inch circle in the flour. Combine nuts, cornstarch, cinnamon, and all but 2 tablespoons of the sugar in a bowl.

5. Whip the egg whites to a light fluff, sprinkle on the 2 reserved tablespoons of sugar, then continue beating until they form firm, glossy peaks.

6. Fold the nut mixture into the egg whites. Scoop the mixture into the center of the traced 12-inch circle and smooth it evenly. Try to leave a small rim at the edge of the circle.

7. Bake the crust for 20 minutes, then remove from the oven and let the crust firm for 5 minutes. Slip a spatula under the crust to make sure it is loose. Let the crust harden on the baking sheet,

then place on a serving platter. (If not to be used within the hour, cover tightly with aluminum foil to keep crisp.)

8. Melt the chocolate over hot water. Set aside.

9. Brush the crust over with the slightly warm raspberry jam. Pour ¾ of the melted chocolate over the jam and spread it evenly, leaving the rim of the crust uncoated.

10. Arrange the drained pear halves on the tart. Brush their tops with melted red currant jelly, just to give them a slight glaze. Drizzle the remaining chocolate over the tops of the pears in a light, lacy pattern. Sprinkle mint leaves and rose flowers in 5 or 6 spots about the tart.

A Chocolate Candy Nest

ere is a pretty, totally edible nest of marzipan and chocolate.

1. Place the chocolate in a small mixing bowl. Put the bowl over warm water and melt the chocolate.

2. Add the marzipan and syrup to the chocolate and mix kneading by hand into a paste until it is uniformly colored.

3. Dust a surface with cocoa. Roll out the paste to about a pasta thickness—no more than ⅛ inch thick. Straighten the edges with the side of a spatula. Using a small, sharp knife, cut ⅓ of the paste into thin strips about ¼ inch wide. Cut the other ⅔ into thinner strips. Run a spatula under the chocolate paste to free the strips.

4. Form the larger strips into the shape of a nest about 4 or 5 inches in diameter. Press the strips

YIELDS A 5-INCH NEST

INGREDIENTS

2 squares semisweet chocolate
7 ounces marzipan or almond paste
2 tablespoons chocolate syrup
Cocoa powder for dusting, preferably Dutch process
Small forked branch with green leaves and/or small ivy stems, rinsed well
Baby's breath, or other small white flower blossoms
Chocolate Truffles (page 147), formed in the shape of small eggs

firmly together to form a solid nest bottom, and build up the sides by pressing and firming the strips into a free-form nest.

5. Place the small branch with green leaves on a large oval platter. (The branch should have a torn look at the end, as if it had broken off a tree.) Place the candy nest amid the greenery. Drape the thinner strips around the rim of the nest to resemble twigs and sticks. Tuck 2 or 3 sprigs of baby's breath around the nest and fill nest with truffles. Guests eat both nest and truffle eggs.

Cakes

A collection of rich, moist cakes—some classics, others exciting new variations on old favorites. Try the German Chocolate Torte, with its intensified chocolate flavoring and its new crisp texture, or the Almond Roca Cake, with thick chunks of chocolate-covered toffee adhering to its frosted surface. Bake these cakes in exciting new shapes and forms: a Coffee Bean so dense with chocolate that it almost is a mousse, a triangular Delta Cake (with more bittersweet buttercream than cake!), or the giant, cream-filled Chocolate Cabbage.

German Chocolate Torte

I find most German chocolate cakes bland and boring, wishy-washy creatures sorely lacking in chocolate backbone. Here is a re-thinking of the standard, with inten-sified chocolate, ground pecans in the batter, and crisp toasted coconut topping for textural relief.

1. Preheat oven to 350 degrees. Grease and flour a 10¼ by 15-inch baking pan.

2. For the cake, melt the chocolate and butter together over hot water. Set aside to cool.

3. Place the sugar, eggs, and vanilla in the bowl of a mixer and beat at medium speed for 12 minutes. The eggs should be very pale and should form wide ribbons when the beaters are raised.

4. While eggs are beating, sift together flour, pecans, salt, and soda.

INGREDIENTS

6 ounces sweet chocolate
1 stick unsalted butter
1½ cups granulated sugar
6 eggs, at room
   temperature
1 teaspoon vanilla extract
1¼ cups sifted all-purpose
   flour
1 cup ground pecans
1 teaspoon salt
¼ teaspoon baking soda
¾ cup buttermilk

TOPPING

4 ounces sweet chocolate
1 cup heavy cream
1 teaspoon vanilla extract
8 ounces shredded
   coconut, lightly toasted
1 cup chopped pecans
14 to 16 large whole
   pecans

5. Alternately add the butter-milk and the chocolate mixture to the dry ingredients, then carefully fold in the beaten eggs until every-thing is just mixed.

6. Pour the batter into the prepared pan and bake for around 30 minutes or until a cake tester comes out clean. Cool the cake on a cake rack.

7. When cake is completely cold, cut in half across the width, and turn out the 2 halves. Place 1 layer on your cake platter. Set the other aside.

8. To make the topping, melt the chocolate over warm water. Let the chocolate cool somewhat, then—using an electric hand mix-er—slowly add the cream. Beat con-tinuously until the mixture is as thick as whipped cream. Flavor with vanilla.

9. Spread some of the filling on the bottom layer of the cake. Sprinkle on some toasted coconut and half the chopped pecans. Top with the remaining cake layer (trim the top to flatten it if necessary).

10. Coat the cake with the chocolate cream mixture. Arrange a 1½-inch wide border of toasted coconut around the top edge. Place the whole pecans in a row around the inside coconut border. Leave the center of the cake plain. Press the remaining toasted coconut and chopped pecans into the sides of the cake. Place cake in the refrigerator to chill until needed.

Rich Devil's Food Layer Cake

This is a rich devil's food cake that is perfect for layering. For a truly spectacular presentation, frost the cake with 7-Minute Frosting, then make dark chocolate ivy leaves and stems (see Rose Pudding Twined with Chocolate Ivy, page 42), and trail them about the rim of the cake.

1. Preheat oven to 350 degrees. Butter and flour 2 round 9-inch cake pans.

2. Melt the chocolate and ½ cup water in the top of a double boiler. Let cool.

3. Cream the butter, sugar, and brown sugar together until light and fluffy (around 5 minutes). Add the vanilla and the eggs, 1 at a time. Beat well after each addition. Beat in the chocolate and mix well.

4. Sift together the flour, soda, and salt. Add flour to the bat-

SERVES 10

INGREDIENTS

4 ounces unsweetened
   chocolate
½ cup water
1 stick unsalted butter
1 cup granulated sugar
½ cup light brown sugar
1 teaspoon vanilla extract
2 eggs
2 cups sifted all-purpose
   flour
1 teaspoon baking soda
¼ teaspoon salt
⅔ cup sweet or sour milk

ter, alternating with milk; stir by hand just until the batter is completely blended.

5. Bake the cakes for 30 to 35 minutes, or until a tester inserted at the center comes out clean. Let cakes cool on racks.

6. Turn out the layers and allow to cool while you prepare the frosting.

7. Melt the chocolate over hot water, then allow to cool.

8. Place egg whites, sugar, cream of tartar, cold water, and salt in the top of a double boiler. Beat with an electric hand mixer for 1 minute.

9. Place the pan over steaming hot water (but not boiling), and continue beating for around 7 minutes, or until mixture is very thick and fluffy. Off the heat, fold in

by hand the vanilla and the melted chocolates.

10.   Place 1 cake layer on your serving dish and coat with frosting. Place on second layer and top with more frosting. Coat sides of cake as well. If desired, twine the chocolate ivy leaves and stems around the top edge.

NOTE

Both layers can be sliced in half further to make 4 layers. If 4 layers are to be frosted, the frosting recipe should be increased by half or even doubled, depending on how much you like frosting.

7-MINUTE FROSTING

2 ounces semisweet chocolate
1 ounce unsweetened chocolate
2 egg whites
1 1/2 cups granulated sugar
1/4 teaspoon cream of tartar
1/3 cup cold water
Pinch salt
1 teaspoon vanilla extract

Delta Cake

A moist, buttery, nut-filled pound cake provides a base for this striking triangular pastry. Lovers of rich, bittersweet buttercream should also approve, for the pastry has more frosting than cake! Note that the cake should be made the night before it is to be cut and assembled.

1. Preheat oven to 325 degrees. Butter and flour a 9 by 5-inch metal loaf pan, preferably with straight sides. (Mirro makes one.)

2. In the bowl of an electric mixer, cream together the butter, sugar, and vanilla. Let the machine run a full 8 minutes so the butter becomes very fluffy. Slow the machine, add 1 egg, then increase the speed and beat for 2 minutes. Continue in this manner adding 1 egg at a time and beating well after each addition.

3. Sift the flour and cornstarch together. Stir in the nuts. Re-

SERVES 18 TO 20

INGREDIENTS

2 sticks unsalted butter, softened
1 cup granulated sugar
1 tablespoon vanilla extract
5 eggs, at room temperature
1 cup sifted all-purpose flour
1/4 cup cornstarch
3/4 cup (tightly packed) roasted, peeled, and ground hazelnuts
2 tablespoons water

move the bowl from the mixer and gently stir in the dry mixture in 3 portions, adding a tablespoon of water between each portion. When the batter is well mixed, pour it into the prepared loaf pan and smooth the top.

4. Place cake in the oven and bake for 1 hour. Put a sheet of aluminum foil loosely over the top, then continue baking cake for another 20 to 30 minutes, or until a cake tester inserted in the center comes out clean.

5. Remove cake from the oven and place pan on a rack (keep on the foil). Let cake cool for 20 minutes, during which time the slightly raised center should settle nicely. Turn the cake out onto a rack. Leave the cake upside down and cover tightly with foil. Leave overnight before cutting and assembling.

6. To prepare the buttercream filling, melt the chocolate over hot water. Set aside.

7. Place butter in the bowl of a mixer and cream it. Add the sugar in 4 or 5 portions, beating well after each addition. Add vanilla, then let butter beat at a high speed for 3 minutes. It will become very pale. (It will be necessary to scrape down the sides of the bowl frequently while making this frosting.)

8. Add the eggs, 1 at a time, and beat for 2 minutes after each addition.

9. Stir cocoa and instant coffee into the melted chocolate. Add the chocolate into buttercream, mix, then add rum and salt. Give the buttercream a final stir with a rubber spatula, so that any butter adhering to the bottom of the bowl will be incorporated.

BITTERSWEET BUTTERCREAM

6 ounces bittersweet chocolate, preferably Tobler Extra-Bittersweet
3 sticks unsalted butter, softened
1½ cups confectioners' sugar, sifted after measuring
2 teaspoons vanilla extract
3 eggs, at room temperature
3 tablespoons cocoa powder, preferably Dutch process
1 teaspoon instant coffee powder
2 teaspoons dark rum (optional)
Large pinch salt

10. If the cake has been baked in a pan with slanted sides, cut off the angled portions so the sides are perfectly straight. With the top of the cake down on a counter, use a long bread knife to gently saw and cut the golden crust from the cake's bottom. Also cut the golden top crust off. Cut the cake horizontally into 7 layers. (Place some division lines at the end of the cake as guidelines.) The cake is firm and handles easily. Trim the layers so that all are same thickness.

11. Place 1 layer on a platter and frost it. The frosting should be made as thick as the cake layer and spread as evenly as possible. Continue layering and frosting the remaining layers, but do *not* frost the top layer. Place cake in freezer and freeze for 1 hour (this is a must).

12. Remove the cake from the freezer and thickly frost the top. Using a long bread knife, cut the cake

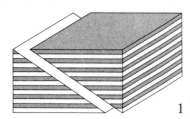

1

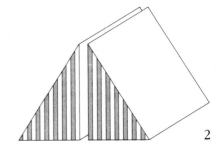

2

diagonally from top to bottom corner (see drawing 1). Press the 2 full sides of the cake together (one is the just frosted,top), so that the cake resembles a triangle, with alternating bands of light and dark running vertically up and down.

13.   Frost the slanting sides of the cake. (You can, if you wish, draw a pastry comb along the sides.) Trim both ends of the cake to expose a neat vertical pattern (2). Place the cake in the freezer. When the exterior frosting is firm, tip the cake and frost the bottom. Let harden.

14.   Place the cake on a serving platter. If desired, use extra buttercream to pipe a row of small rosettes along the apex or around the edge. Place cake in refrigerator until needed, then cut into thin cross sections to serve.

Chocolate Buttermilk Cake with Sour Cream Frosting

This is a very dark, moist cake with a light filling and frosting of sour cream.

1. Preheat oven to 350 degrees. Butter a 10-inch springform pan. Line the bottom with a round of wax or parchment paper and lightly butter the paper.

2. In the bowl of an electric mixer, cream together the butter and sugar until light and fluffy. Add the eggs, 1 at a time, and continue beating until thick and light.

3. Sieve together the cocoa, baking soda, baking powder, cinnamon, and flour. With the mixer on low speed, add the dry ingredients in 4 portions, alternating with the buttermilk and coffee. Beat until perfectly blended.

4. Pour batter into the prepared pan and bake for 60 minutes, or until a cake tester comes out

SERVES 10 TO 12

INGREDIENTS

2 sticks unsalted butter, softened
1½ cups granulated sugar
2 eggs
½ cup cocoa powder
1 teaspoon baking soda
1 teaspoon baking powder
1 teaspoon ground cinnamon
2 cups sifted all-purpose flour
1½ cups buttermilk
1 tablespoon instant coffee powder, dissolved in 1 tablespoon hot water

SOUR CREAM FROSTING

1 cup sour cream
1 cup confectioners' sugar, sifted after measuring
1 cup heavy cream

clean. Run a knife or spatula around the edge of the cake. Let the cake cool completely in the pan.

5. Make the frosting shortly before needed. Mix together the sour cream and the sugar. Whip the heavy cream until it is firm, then mix the 2 creams together.

6. Release the cake and turn it out upside down on a platter. Use a long serrated knife to cut the cake into layers. Spread the frosting generously over one layer and top with the other layer. Swirl the filling over the entire top and sides of the cake. Refrigerate until ready to serve.

Sour Cream Marbled Pound Cake

A good, moist cake with hand-some dark-chocolate marblings. The cake forms its own crisp sugared crust—no topping is necessary.

1. Preheat oven to 325 degrees. Butter a Bundt, kugelhopf or 10-inch tube pan well. Add a large scoop of sugar to the pan and rotate it until all interior surfaces are generously coated. Gently tap out excess, but allow as much sugar as possible to adhere, for this is what forms the good outer crust.

2. Melt chocolate over hot water.

3. Cream the butter and sugar in the bowl of an electric mixer until the mixture is very thick and pale, at least 6 minutes. Beat in the eggs 1 at a time, with a full minute's beating after each addition.

4. Sift together the flour, salt, and baking soda. With the machine

SERVES 12

INGREDIENTS

6 ounces semisweet chocolate
2 sticks unsalted butter, softened
2½ cups granulated sugar
6 eggs
3 cups sifted all-purpose flour
¼ teaspoon salt
¼ teaspoon baking soda
1 cup sour cream
2 teaspoons vanilla extract
1 tablespoon almond extract

running at low speed, add the dry ingredients alternating with the sour cream. Add the vanilla and almond extracts. Remove bowl from machine, give a final stir with a spatula to catch any ingredients remaining at the bottom of the bowl, then pour slightly over half the batter into pan.

5. Add the melted chocolate to the remaining batter and stir until blended. Spoon the chocolate batter onto the white and, with each spoonful, cut down and swirl the chocolate through. Place cake in oven and bake for 1 hour, or until a tester inserted at cake center comes out clean. Remove and cool briefly on a rack before unmolding.

6. Run a knife around the edge of the cake and turn it out onto a serving platter. Cut thin slices; best served the day after it is made.

Chocolate Sponge Cake

A basic recipe for a rich and moist chocolate sponge cake. It is adaptable to all sorts of shapes and fillable with any good thing one can imagine.

1. Preheat oven to 350 degrees. Butter and flour a 10-inch springform pan, or 2 layer cake pans 8 inches in diameter. Place pans on a cookie sheet.

2. Place eggs, sugar, and vanilla in the metal bowl of an electric mixer. Hold the bowl over low heat and, stirring the ingredients with your hand, mix until the eggs are just warm and the sugar has melted. (If your mixer doesn't have a metal bowl, use a glass one and heat mixture over hot water.) Place the bowl on the mixer and beat at medium speed for 9 minutes. The mixture should be very thick and quadrupled in size.

SERVES 12 TO 15

INGREDIENTS

7 eggs plus 2 egg yolks
1 cup granulated sugar
1 teaspoon vanilla extract
1 cup sifted all-purpose
  flour
2/3 cup cocoa powder
1/4 teaspoon salt
3 tablespoons unsalted
  butter, melted

3. Sift together the flour, cocoa, and salt. Add the dry mixture to the eggs in 3 portions, folding them in by hand. Hold your fingers spread stiffly apart and gently lift and turn the batter until you can feel the perfect amalgamation of ingredients. Rapidly fold in butter, then scoop the batter into the prepared pan.

4. Place the cake in the oven and bake for 30 to 40 minutes (depending on size of container), or until a toothpick inserted in the center of the cake comes out clean. Remove from oven and cool briefly.

5. Unmold the cake and frost, glaze, or serve plain with whipped cream.

Chocolate Cabbage Cake

This cake is the pièce de résistance of the book. Bake a sponge cake in 2 round bowls and sandwich the halves together with whipped cream. Mold chocolate leaves from a real cabbage, place them around the cake, then present guests with the prettiest knock-em-dead creation they have ever seen.

1. Preheat oven to 350 degrees. Butter and flour the mixing bowls. Place bowls on a cookie sheet.

2. Prepare the Chocolate Sponge Cake batter. Divide the batter between the 2 mixing bowls and smooth the tops evenly. Place sheet with bowls in the oven. Bake for 30 to 35 minutes, or until a toothpick inserted in the centers comes out clean. Remove cakes and let cool for 5 minutes. They should shrink slightly away from the sides of the pans, and then they will unmold eas-

SERVES 15 TO 20

INGREDIENTS

1 recipe Chocolate Sponge Cake (page 61)
Rum, Grand Marnier, or crème de cacao (optional)
1 cup heavy cream, whipped stiff and sweetened and flavored to taste
1 pound semisweet or compound chocolate
8 leaves green cabbage (not savoy)
2 1½-quart stainless-steel mixing bowls, 8 inches round
2 or 3 pale pink rose buds

ily. Leave to cool completely. The cakes should be allowed to firm at least 3 hours for best results.

3. Hollow out a portion from the flat center side of each cake. Sprinkle the cakes with optional liquor, then crumble the dug-out portions. Whip and flavor the cream, then stir in the cake crumbs. Refill the hollowed centers of the cakes and sandwich them together. This round ball will be the head of the cabbage. Refrigerate until needed.

4. Melt chocolate over warm water. Set aside.

5. Coat the backs of 5 nice cabbage leaves with chocolate by spreading it on with a pastry brush. Brush chocolate to within ¼ inch of the leaves' edges. Coat the top side of 3 other leaves, upper half of the leaf only.

6. Leave 1 fully coated leaf flat and drape the others over small

bowls so they will harden in slightly rounded shapes. Refrigerate leaves for 8 minutes.

7. If any chocolate has dripped over the unpainted sides of the leaves, chip it off. Loosen the fat stem end first, then gently work the cabbage leaf off the chocolate. As long as you have 3 good whole leaves you are all right, for broken halves can also be used effectively.

8. Prepare glaze by putting chocolate, sugar, corn syrup, and hot water in a saucepan, then cook over medium-low heat, stirring constantly. Let the mixture cook at a slow boil for 3 minutes. Off the heat, stir in the butter 1 tablespoon at a time, then add the vanilla and confectioners' sugar. Stir until the glaze cools slightly and is a nice spreading consistency.

9. When glaze is somewhat cool and thick enough to swirl into a

THICK CHOCOLATE GLAZE

4 ounces semisweet chocolate chips or grated squares
1/2 cup granulated sugar
1/4 cup light corn syrup
1/4 cup hot water
5 tablespoons unsalted butter
1 teaspoon vanilla extract
4 to 5 tablespoons confectioners' sugar

pattern, coat 1 side of the round cake. Set 3 large leaves on a platter and place the frosted side of the cake on top of them.

10. Glaze the top of the cake, then press other leaves around the sides; let a few small broken portions suggest a gathering of leaves atop the cabbage. Let the glaze firm. Tuck the roses about the cake.

11. To serve, cut portions from the round cake. The bottom leaves can be nibbled on with coffee or removed and used for another recipe.

Chocolate Raspberry Torte

A spectacular torte that looks like a large chocolate raspberry flower.

1. Preheat oven to 350 degrees. The thinner and larger this torte can be made, the prettier it will be. It can be made in a 10-inch cake pan, but if you have one, use a large, sided pizza pan (mine is 12 inches across at the bottom). Generously butter and flour the baking pan. Pour in the cake batter and bake in oven for 25 minutes, or until the cake tests firm in the middle. Let the cake cool 5 minutes, then turn it out and let it cool and firm up completely for at least 2 hours.

2. Slice the cake into 2 layers with a long, serrated knife. Sprinkle the inside of each layer generously with liquor, then spread raspberry jam over each half. Spread the bottom layer of the cake with buttercream, then reassemble the cake.

SERVES 10 TO 12

INGREDIENTS

1 recipe Chocolate Sponge Cake batter (page 61)
Framboise or light rum
1/3 cup raspberry jam (approximately), melted
1/2 recipe Bittersweet Buttercream (page 57), made with 1 egg plus 1 egg yolk
2 cups fresh raspberries, approximately

LEAVES

4 ounces semisweet or bittersweet chocolate
12 to 15 plain rose or other flat oval leaves (enough to surround the cake)

(Note: if the top layer of the cake is not perfectly smooth, trim it flat, then turn the cake over and use the smooth bottom of the cake as the top.) Place cake in refrigerator to chill.

3. To make the chocolate leaves, melt the chocolate over hot water. Coat the *back* side of each leaf with the melted chocolate, then carefully wipe off any chocolate that has wended its way to the front of the leaf. Place leaves on a tray and let them harden in the refrigerator for 5 minutes. Peel off leaves from the chocolate, starting from the stem ends.

4. To make the glaze, combine butter and corn syrup in a saucepan. Stirring constantly, bring to a simmer over low heat, then continue simmering and stirring for 1 minute. Remove from heat and add chocolate and liquor. Whisk until the choc-

olate has melted and the glaze is smooth. Let cool for 8 minutes, then pour and spread glaze over the top and sides of the cake.

5. Press the raspberries into the central portion of the cake and insert the chocolate leaves in a flower shape in the middle. Fill the hollow with raspberries.

6. Place cake in refrigerator for at least 1 hour or until needed. This cake can be composed in the morning and eaten the following night, but once it is glazed and berried, it is best consumed that same day.

CHOCOLATE GLAZE

5 tablespoons unsalted butter

4 tablespoons light corn syrup

5 ounces bittersweet chocolate, grated or chopped

1 tablespoon famboise or light rum

Almond Roca Cake

A delicious cake with rough and rugged good looks, for its chocolate frosted exterior is coated with chunks of broken toffee.

1. Preheat oven to 350 degrees. Butter and flour a 9-inch tube or Bundt pan.

2. Place eggs, yolks, and sugars in the metal bowl of an electric mixer. Place bowl over low heat and stir the eggs with your hand until the mixture becomes warm and you can feel that the sugar crystals have dissolved. (If your mixer does not have a metal bowl, use a glass one and place it over hot water.) Place bowl on machine and beat for 10 minutes at medium speed. The eggs should be very thick and form a heavy ribbon.

3. Add the almonds, vanilla and almond extracts, and zest to the eggs, and beat briefly.

INGREDIENTS

6 eggs plus 2 egg yolks
1/4 cup granulated sugar
1/2 cup brown sugar, tightly packed
1/2 cup ground toasted almonds
1 teaspoon vanilla extract
1/4 teaspoon almond extract
1 teaspoon finely grated lemon zest
1 cup sifted all-purpose flour
1/4 teaspoon salt
3 tablespoons unsalted butter, melted and lightly browned

4. By hand, fold in the flour and salt in 3 portions. Work rapidly and gently so as not to deflate the egg volume. Drizzle on the browned butter and fold it in.

5. Pour the batter into the prepared pan, place pan on a cookie sheet, and put cake in the oven. Bake for 35 minutes, or until the cake shrinks slightly from the side of the pan and a cake tester comes out clean when inserted at a central point. Let cool for 10 minutes, then unmold cake onto a rack. Let cool completely.

6. To prepare the syrup, bring the sugar and water to a simmer in a small saucepan. Let simmer 3 minutes, then remove from the heat and cool briefly. Stir in Amaretto liqueur.

7. Make glaze and chill to spreading consistency.

8. Slice the cake in half horizontally through the center and drizzle the hot syrup over the cut sides. Let cool, then spread on chocolate glaze.

9. Reform cake and smooth glaze on in a rough fashion, then press the broken portions of toffee over the surface. Let the glaze cool and harden. Serve with whipped cream.

SYRUP

⅓ cup granulated sugar
½ cup water
Amaretto to taste (at least 2 tablespoons)
1 recipe Thick Chocolate Glaze (page 63)
16 to 20 ounces Almond Roca or Chocolate Covered Macadamia Nut Toffee (page 156) made with almonds, or other purchased chocolate-covered nut toffee, broken into small bits, some as large as 1 inch square
Whipped cream

Chocolate Pound Cake

In its traditional tubular form, the best pound cake I've ever tasted.

1. Preheat oven to 325 degrees. Butter and flour a 10-inch tube pan.

2. Sift together the cocoa, flour, baking powder, salt, and instant coffee, and set aside.

3. This cake is most easily made using an electric mixer. Cream the butter in the mixer bowl until it is fluffy. Continue beating and add the sugar in a slow stream. Beat at a high speed for 5 minutes. Slow mixer, then add the vanilla. Add the eggs, 1 at a time, beating briefly after each addition.

4. Mix in dry ingredients alternating with the liquid, starting and ending with dry ingredients. Scrape down the mixer bowl as necessary.

5. When the batter is well blended, pour it into the prepared

SERVES 12 TO 15

INGREDIENTS

1 cup cocoa powder
2 cups sifted all-purpose flour
1/2 teaspoon baking powder
1 teaspoon salt
2 tablespoons instant coffee powder
3 sticks unsalted butter
3 cups granulated sugar
2 teaspoons vanilla extract
5 eggs
1 cup buttermilk
1/4 cup water

tube pan and bake in the upper third of the oven for 1 hour and 20 minutes, or until a cake tester comes out clean.

6. Let cake rest in the pan for 20 minutes, then unmold onto a cake rack. Let cool completely before serving. This cake stays moist for days.

Chocolate Coffee Bean Cake

1. Preheat oven to 325 degrees. Prepare the batter for Chocolate Pound Cake. Grease and flour a 3-quart, round 9-inch metal bowl.

2. Pour the batter in and bake in the lower third of the oven for 2 hours and 30 minutes (yes, that's correct). Halfway through the baking time, cover the bowl with aluminum foil. A thin crisp crust should rise and form over the cake.

3. Remove cake from oven and let sit for 1 hour. Remove the pieces of crust and set aside for decoration. Turn out the cake onto a rack and let cool overnight.

4. To form a coffee bean, use a serrated knife to cut the cake into 2 layers horizontally. The small, bottom-of-the-bowl layer is the bottom of the coffee bean cake. Spread its cut side with frosting. Cut the top layer across in 2 semicircles. Place them on top of the frosted layer,

SERVES 12 TO 15

INGREDIENTS

1 recipe Chocolate Pound Cake batter (page 68)
½ recipe Cocoa Frosting (page 107)
Sweetened whipped cream
Chocolate-covered coffee bean candy (available at gourmet stores)

leaving a ¾-inch division between the 2 halves like the split down the center of a coffee bean.

5. Arrange the broken pieces of crisp crust over the top of the cake and dust the top lightly with confectioners' sugar. Place the cake on a serving tray and pipe some whipped cream in large rosettes around the bottom. Top each rosette with a chocolate-covered coffee bean. Serve with good, strong coffee.

White Chocolate Gâteau

A curious and delicate cake. There is, I think, almost a taste of coconut within the layers, and the buttercream in copious quantity will delight lovers of white chocolate.

1. Preheat oven to 375 degrees. Lightly butter a 15½ by 10¼-inch jellyroll pan. Line pan with parchment paper, then butter and flour the paper.

2. Melt the white chocolate over hot water.

3. In the bowl of an electric mixer, cream together the butter and sugar. Continuously beating, add the egg yolks, 1 at a time, and beat until the mixture is very thick. Slow the machine down, add the melted white chocolate and crème de cacao, and mix just until blended. By hand, stir in the ground almonds and graham cracker crumbs.

SERVES 12 TO 15

INGREDIENTS

8 ounces white chocolate, grated then melted
1 stick unsalted butter, softened
1 cup granulated sugar
8 eggs, separated and at room temperature
¼ cup crème de cacao
1 cup ground blanched almonds
1 cup fine graham cracker crumbs
Confectioners' sugar

WHITE CHOCOLATE BUTTERCREAM

8 ounces white chocolate, grated
1 cup granulated sugar
3 tablespoons cornstarch
½ cup boiling water
¼ cup crème de cacao
3 sticks unsalted butter, softened

4. Beat the egg whites until they form stiff but not dry peaks. Stir ⅓ of the whites into the yolk mixture to lighten it, then fold in the remaining whites.

5. Rapidly spread the mixture onto the prepared pan and smooth it lightly. Bake for 30 minutes, or until a cake tester inserted in the center comes out clean. Remove from oven and let cool briefly.

6. Place a kitchen towel on a counter and dust it lightly with confectioners' sugar. Flip the cake over onto the towel. Peel off the parchment paper, then let the cake cool completely.

7. For the buttercream, combine white chocolate, sugar, and cornstarch in a saucepan. Mix, then add the boiling water and stir over low heat just until the mixture thickens. Let cool briefly, then stir in

crème de cacao and continue cooling to room temperature.

8. Place butter in a mixer and cream it for 5 minutes. Gradually add the white chocolate mixture to the butter and continue beating until all is smooth.

9. Cut the cake into 2 long strips *or* 3 crosswise strips, and trim them evenly. Sandwich and frost the layers with buttercream. Pipe a decorative border of buttercream around the top and bottom of the cake if you wish. Chill until firm before serving.

Chocolate Baumkuchen

Baumkuchen *(log cake)*, is a German specialty that is rarely made these days. Traditionally, a spit was arranged before an open fire. Batter was poured over the spit, and as the spit slowly rotated, the batter cooked and hardened. More batter was poured on and soon a series of thin, concentric rings formed, like those you see patterned on a cut tree stump. This easy, modern adaptation has 4 thin layers firmed under the broiler, then rolled into a log. It puts a simple jellyroll to shame.

1. Oil or grease a 15½ by 10¼-inch jellyroll pan. Set aside.

2. Beat the egg yolks in the bowl of an electric mixer until thick and pale (around 8 minutes). Cream the butter and ¾ cup of sugar until light and fluffy. Slowly beat the yolks into the butter mixture. Add the vanilla and mix until well blended.

SERVES 12 TO 15

INGREDIENTS

10 eggs, separated
1½ sticks unsalted butter
1 cup granulated sugar
1 teaspoon vanilla extract
1 teaspoon instant coffee
  powder
2 tablespoons cocoa
  powder
1 cup sifted all-purpose
  flour
⅓ cup cornstarch
Large pinch salt
Light rum or cognac
  (optional)

FILLING

1 pound semisweet
  chocolate chips
1 stick butter
2 tablespoons water
Instant coffee powder

3. Sieve the coffee, cocoa, flour, cornstarch, and salt into a mixing bowl. Stir into the egg mixture by hand.

4. Preheat the broiler.

5. Beat the egg whites in a clean, grease-free bowl. When they have formed soft peaks, sprinkle on the remaining ¼ cup of sugar and continue beating until they form firm but not dry peaks. Stir a large spoon of the whites into the yolk mixture, then fold in the remaining whites.

6. Spread ¼ of the batter into the oiled jellyroll pan. Smooth it as evenly as possible, then place pan 5 to 6 inches under the broiler. Let cook around 1 minute. Turn the pan about as necessary to make sure that the entire surface is firm and lightly browned. A few light brown speckles may appear, but do not let the cake over-crisp at any point.

7. Remove cake from the heat; run a knife around the edge of the cake. In about a minute, the cake should lift easily from one end of the pan. Turn the pan over and gently let the cake drop loose from the pan. Reoil the pan and continue making another cake layer. There will be 4 layers in all. If you can manage it, start the filling as the cakes cook.

8. Place half the chocolate chips and 4 tablespoons of the butter in a pan over hot water. Add water and let the chocolate melt. Stir to a smooth, easily spreadable glaze (a bit more water can be added as needed). Stir in some coffee to taste (I like a strong flavoring essence here).

9. Spread the filling over the first cake layer. Roll up, starting with the short edge. Continue frosting and rolling the remaining layers. Finally the log will be a good 5 inches

BARK AND TOPPING

3 to 4 ounces semisweet or
  compound chocolate
Confectioners' sugar
Whipped cream

wide and have around 14 concentric rings. Make up and use more chocolate filling as you need it. (It tends to dry fast, which is why you make it in 2 batches.) Frost the entire outside of the cake except for one end.

10. To make bark, melt the chocolate over hot water. Stir briefly until smooth, then pour out onto a counter or marble slab. Run a long flexible spatula back and forth over the chocolate, spreading, smoothing, and working it just until the chocolate loses its gloss and turns flat in color. With the edge of the spatula or a large chef's knife, angle into the chocolate and scrape along, turning up large rolls of chocolate in rough barklike sections.

11. Cut off the unfrosted end of the cake at a slight slant to reveal the ringed pattern. Arrange the chocolate bark parallel to cake over the

surface and mainly on top. Let the frosting harden.

12. Sieve just a bit of confectioners' sugar directly over the top of the cake, then transfer the log to a doily-covered serving platter. Lightly whipped cream is a necessary accompaniment to the baumkuchen.

Craters of the Moon Cake

This cake is especially for children. Make "craters" in the dry ingredients, pour in liquids, and watch the vinegar lake foam and bubble. Scatter marshmallows on the surface, and the round moon cake will have a rocky, pitted surface.

1. Preheat the oven to 350 degrees.

2. Take a 9- or 10-inch cake pan and put flour, sugars, salt, and cocoa right in the pan. Mix carefully. When you have stirred it very well, you will have the light brown moon sand.

3. Take a spoon and make a big crater in the center so the bottom of the pan shows through. Make a medium-sized crater elsewhere in the sand, and another little crater on the other side. Spoon baking soda into medium-sized crater.

SERVES 6 TO 8

INGREDIENTS

1½ cups sifted all-purpose flour
½ cup granulated sugar
½ cup brown sugar
1 teaspoon salt
4 tablespoons cocoa powder
5 tablespoons butter, melted
1 teaspoon vanilla extract
1 teaspoon baking soda
1 tablespoon white vinegar
1 cup milk
⅔ cup miniature marshmallows

4. Pour the melted butter into the large crater. Pour the vanilla into the smallest crater. Pour the vinegar into the medium-sized crater and watch how it becomes a bubbling, foaming volcano. When the volcano stops foaming, pour the milk over the moon sand and carefully mix everything together until it looks like smooth mud.

5. Scatter marshmallow rocks over the surface.

6. Bake for around 35 minutes, or until a toothpick stuck in the cake's center comes out dry. Let the cake cool in the pan.

7. Cut portions of moon and serve directly from baking dish.

Chocolate Strawberry Shortcake

A nice summer's dessert. Keep this chocolate shortcake chilling in the refrigerator until needed, then carry out the pretty display at the end of a warm day's lunch or supper.

1. Preheat oven to 400 degrees. Butter 2 round 10-inch cake pans.

2. Sift together the cocoa, flour, baking soda, salt, baking powder, and sugar into a bowl. Add the chilled butter and cut it into the dry ingredients with a pastry cutter or your fingertips. When the mixture resembles oatmeal, sprinkle on the buttermilk and milk and lightly pack the dough into a ball. Divide dough in half.

3. Roll out each portion of dough on a floured surface, then pack and press it gently into the baking tins. Sprinkle the top of one cake with the mixed granulated and

SERVES 8

INGREDIENTS

5 tablespoons cocoa
    powder
2 cups sifted all-purpose
    flour
½ teaspoon baking soda
½ teaspoon salt
1 tablespoon baking
    powder
½ cup granulated sugar
1 stick unsalted butter,
    chilled and cut into
    small pieces
½ cup buttermilk
½ cup milk
2 tablespoons granulated
    sugar mixed with 1
    tablespoon light brown
    sugar for topping
3 pints strawberries, rinsed
Granulated sugar as
    needed

(continued)

brown sugar and dash a few drops of cold water over the sugar.

4. Bake cakes for 15 minutes in the hot oven. Remove cakes, cool them briefly, then turn out onto racks and let cool completely.

5. Select 10 of the largest strawberries and set them aside whole and unhulled. Hull and coarsely chop the remaining berries and sugar them to taste. Refrigerate strawberry sauce until needed.

6. Melt chocolate over hot water. Set aside.

7. Line a baking sheet with wax paper.

8. Dip or brush the bottom half of each whole berry in the chocolate. Place the berries on a tray and refrigerate until needed.

9. Fit a pastry bag with a large, plain nozzle.

10. To prepare the cream filling, place gelatin and cold water in a Pyrex measuring cup. Place cup in a saucepan containing an inch of water and heat gently until the gelatin melts.

11. Place cream and vanilla in a bowl and beat until the cream has thickened slightly. Stir 2 tablespoons of the cream into the warm gelatin and quickly add mixture to the cream. Resume beating immediately. Sprinkle on the confectioners' sugar and continue beating until the cream is thick.

12. Spoon ¼ of the cream into the pastry bag; set aside. Spread a lot of the remaining cream on top of the bottom cake layer and top with some chopped strawberries. Put other cake layer on top. Place on serving dish. (An especially effective one would be a glass cake stand covered with large green leaves.)

2 ounces bittersweet or semisweet chocolate
Hot Fudge Sauce (page 172), cooled and thinned to a pouring consistency (optional)

FILLING

1 teaspoon unflavored gelatin
1½ tablespoons cold water
1½ cups heavy cream
1 teaspoon vanilla extract
¼ cup confectioners' sugar, or to taste

13. Place more chopped strawberries on top, then pipe 5 large swirls of cream around the top edge. Pipe 5 more swirls around the bottom edge. The cake can be refrigerated at this point for an hour or so.

14. Top each dollop of cream with a chocolate-dipped strawberry and drizzle with fudge sauce, if desired. Serve the strawberry sauce on the side.

Lenzer Torte

A rapidly executed, very adult cake. Keep an extra can of tart cherries on hand and, with the remaining ingredients as commonly kept staples, you will have a good emergency dessert that can fit even the most elegant occasion.

1. Preheat oven to 325 degrees. Butter the bottom and sides of a 9-inch springform pan. Place the bread crumbs on the bottom of the pan and rotate the pan until the crumbs evenly cover the bottom. Set aside.

2. Drain the cherries well and place them on paper toweling until needed.

3. Beat the eggs and sugar together until thick and lemon colored. Stir in the melted butter, cocoa, and vanilla. Mix well, then fold in the flour, baking powder, and nuts.

SERVES 6

INGREDIENTS

2 tablespoons fine bread crumbs
1 can (1 pound) pitted tart cherries (available at gourmet produce stores), well drained
2 eggs
1 cup granulated sugar
1 stick unsalted butter, melted
3 tablespoons cocoa powder
½ teaspoon vanilla extract
½ cup all-purpose flour, sifted after measuring
1 teaspoon baking powder
½ cup walnuts, finely chopped
Confectioners' sugar
Whipped cream, sweetened to taste and well chilled

4. Scatter the cherries over the bottom of the prepared pan. Pour the batter over the cherries and place pan in the oven. Bake for 50 to 55 minutes or until the top of the cake feels completely firm.

5. Remove from oven and let cool for 10 minutes. Run a knife around the edge of the pan and release the springform siding. Let the cake sit until completely cool.

6. Place a plate on top of the cake and turn both cake and plate carefully over. Run a long, thin knife or spatula under the springform bottom and lift it off. Place a serving platter over the soft, cherried bottom and reverse both plates so that the cake is right side up.

7. Sift a bit of confectioners' sugar over the cake's surface (which will not be perfectly smooth, by the way). Serve the cake with chilled whipped cream on the side.

Sacher Torte

A well-known Austrian confection, with a slick glaze of bittersweet chocolate and a hidden layer of apricot jam.

1. Preheat oven to 350 degrees. Butter and flour a 10-inch springform pan.

2. Melt the chocolate over warm water, and keep warm.

3. Sift together the almonds, salt, and flour. Set aside.

4. Place the egg yolks in the bowl of a mixer. Beat until pale yellow, then add half the sugar and continue beating until very thick. Turn the mixer to low speed, then add the melted chocolate.

5. Beat the egg whites until they begin to stiffen, then add the remaining sugar, 1 tablespoon at a time, and continue beating until the whites are very stiff and glossy.

SERVES 10

INGREDIENTS

6 ounces unsweetened
  chocolate
⅓ cup ground almonds
Pinch salt
1 cup sifted all-purpose
  flour
8 eggs, separated
1 cup confectioners' sugar
5 tablespoons unsalted
  butter, melted
1 tablespoon amaretto or
  light rum
⅔ cup smooth apricot jam,
  approximately (purée or
  strain if necessary)
1 recipe Chocolate Glaze
  (page 63)

6. Combine the butter and amaretto or rum. Fold the dry ingredients and egg whites alternately and gently into the chocolate mixture. Drizzle on the melted butter and continue folding only until batter is smooth. Do not overwork.

7. Pour at once into the prepared cake pan, and gently smooth the top. Bake cake for 50 to 60 minutes, or until a cake tester comes out clean. Remove and let cool.

8. Firm the cake for 30 minutes in the freezer before cutting. Slice the cake carefully into 2 horizontal layers with a bread knife. Spread the bottom layer with apricot jam, then cover with the remaining layer. Brush jam around sides and over top.

9. Make the glaze as directed, then spread it smoothly over the top and side of the cake. This cake is usually presented with the name "Sacher" piped across the top.

Black Forest Torte

Black Forest Torte, a heady compilation of chocolate cake, cream, Kirsch, and cherries, is built upon the same base that is used for Sacher Torte. Make this cake when fresh black cherries are in season.

1. Bake the cake as in the previous recipe and let it cool. Slice horizontally into 2 layers, and sprinkle each layer generously with Kirsch.

2. Whip the cream very stiff and sweeten it to taste with confectioners' sugar. Mix ⅓ of the cream with 2 cups of the cherries and smooth over 1 cake layer. Top with the remaining cake layer.

3. Swirl the remaining cream around the side and over the top of the cake. Just before serving, scatter the remaining cherry halves over the top and sprinkle with shaved chocolate. Keep cake refrigerated until needed. (As the whipped cream contains no stabilizer, the cake should be consumed within 2 hours for best results.)

SERVES 12

INGREDIENTS

1 recipe Sacher Torte cake base (page 79), flavored with Kirsch instead of amaretto
Kirsch
2½ cups heavy cream
Confectioners' sugar
3 cups fresh black cherries, stemmed, pitted, and cut in half
Shaved or grated bittersweet chocolate

Pastries and Pies

*T*hick fudge tarts heaped with whipped cream mountains. The rich-est chocolate quiche imaginable. Truffle Cupcakes, Cocoa Pota-toes, Chocolate Honeycomb. Sophisticated orange and bittersweet chocolate chess tarts, and designer brownies so good that they need to be crested with your exclusive initials—all impatiently await you in this chapter.

Quick, turn the page!

Napoleon Tart

A lazy person's mille-feuilles: *not as much work; almost the same sensation and splendid looks.*

1. To make the pastry, mix flour and salt in a bowl. Cut chilled butter bits and shortening into the flour with knives or a pastry cutter until the mixture resembles oatmeal. Sprinkle on the ice water until a cohesive dough can be formed. Divide the dough into 3 portions and very briefly knead each portion under the heel of your hand. Pack the dough into a ball, then wrap and chill for at least 30 minutes.

2. On a floured counter, roll out the dough to an approximate 10 by 14-inch rectangle. Give the dough a turn (that is, fold the top edge 2/3 of the way down, and bring the bottom edge up over it to form a triple layer). Turn the dough long way up and again roll out to a rectangle. Fold into thirds. Wrap dough and put to

SERVES 10 TO 12

INGREDIENTS

1 3/4 cups sifted all-purpose
   flour
1 teaspoon salt
1 1/2 sticks unsalted butter,
   chilled and cut into bits
3 tablespoons vegetable
   shortening
1/2 cup ice water,
   approximately
3 ounces semisweet or
   bittersweet chocolate
3 tablespoons unsalted
   butter
Raspberry jam, melted

PASTRY CREAM

3 cups milk
1 cup granulated sugar
8 egg yolks
Scant 1 cup sifted
   all-purpose flour
1 tablespoon plus 1
   teaspoon vanilla extract
2 tablespoons unsalted
   butter, in 1 piece

chill for 30 minutes (or overnight, if you wish).

3. On a lightly floured surface this time roll out 3 circles 11 inches in diameter. Transfer circles to ungreased baking sheets, cover with plastic wrap, and let rest for 15 minutes. Preheat oven to 375 degrees.

4. Prick the dough circles with a fork and bake for 15 to 20 minutes or until nicely golden. Remove from oven and let cool.

5. To make the pastry cream, bring milk to a boil and let cool briefly. Whisk together the sugar and egg yolks. Add the flour and mix to a smooth paste. Slowly stir the milk into the eggs, then return mixture to a clean pan and, stirring continuously, bring to a boil. Remove from heat immediately. Add vanilla. Rub butter over the surface to form a protective coating that will keep the custard

from forming a skin while it cools. Chill, then stir butter into the custard immediately before using.

6. Melt chocolate with butter over hot water.

7. To assemble, choose the pastry layer with the smoothest surface and set it aside. Spread melted chocolate over the bottom of the reserved top layer and over 1 other layer, which will serve as bottom layer. Refrigerate these layers briefly to harden.

8. Place the bottom pastry layer on a platter, chocolate side up. Coat with half the pastry cream. Coat the middle layer of pastry on one side with raspberry jam. Place the jammed side down onto the pastry cream. Coat the top of the middle layer also with jam. Smooth the remaining pastry cream over the jam. Top with the top layer, chocolate side down. Refrigerate to harden.

MARBLE ICING

2 ounces semisweet chocolate chips or grated squares
1½ teaspoons vegetable shortening
1½ cups confectioners' sugar
3 tablespoons light corn syrup
2 tablespoons heavy cream
1 teaspoon vanilla extract
Paper pastry bag (page xviii)

9. Melt the chocolate for the icing and the vegetable shortening in a small pan over hot water.

10. Trim a good-sized thick edge from around the cake so that all the pretty layers make a neat showing.

11. Whisk together the confectioners' sugar, corn syrup, cream, and vanilla and immediately pour the icing over the top of the pastry. Smooth with a palette knife and let it drip down the sides of the tart.

12. Immediately spoon the melted chocolate into the paper pastry bag. Cut off a small tip, then draw 5 or 6 concentric circles on the tart top with the chocolate. From the center point, run a knife back and forth across the pattern, reversing the direction of the knife each time and wiping the blade after each line is drawn. This patterning technique is called feathering or marblizing. If

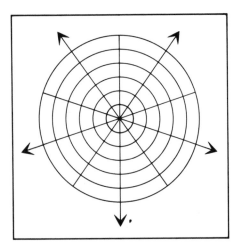

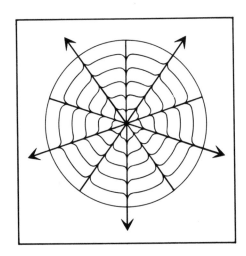

you wish, pipe small rosettes of whipped cream around the bottom edge of the pastry just before serving. This is delicious served with strawberries on the side, best eaten within 2 days of assemblage.

Chocolate Quiche

A very rich, dense chocolate version of a quiche. Serve it in its quiche baking dish.

1. Combine the flour, salt, and almonds in a bowl. Cut the chilled butter into flour with your fingertips until dough resembles oatmeal.

2. Beat the egg yolk with 1 tablespoon of ice water. Sprinkle over the flour and gently work dough until it can be compacted into a neat ball. (Sprinkle on extra water as needed.) Chill for 30 minutes.

3. Preheat the oven to 350 degrees.

4. Generously flour a counter and roll out the dough. Line a standard 11-inch quiche pan with the dough and pinch and press any broken portions together to make a smooth crust. Place a sheet of greased aluminum foil over the dough and fill the crust with dried

SERVES 16

INGREDIENTS

18 ounces semisweet
  chocolate
1¾ cups heavy cream
7 egg yolks

CRUST

¾ cup sifted all-purpose
  flour
Pinch salt
¾ cup ground blanched
  almonds
1 stick plus 2 tablespoons
  unsalted butter, chilled
  and cut into bits
1 egg yolk
Ice water as needed

beans or other weights. Bake blind for 10 minutes, then remove foil and beans and bake for another 3 minutes. Cool.

5. When ready to bake quiche, heat oven to 350 degrees.

6. To make filling, melt chocolate over hot water and cool slightly.

7. In another bowl, beat together the cream and egg yolks until they are well blended. Add the melted chocolate and mix well. Pour the filling into the quiche crust and bake for around 45 minutes. (The top should feel firm though the insides will not test out dry.)

8. Let quiche cool completely before serving. This is nice when just slightly cool but not cold. Serve small portions, and if you wish add a dollop of whipped cream to each.

Chocolate Mocha Cheesecake

I like to serve this mildly tart and delicious cheesecake within 24 hours after it has baked so that the sugary top remains crisp.

1.   Butter the sides of a 10-inch springform pan. Cut a 10-inch circle of wax paper and fit it into the bottom of the pan.

2.   To make the crust, mix cookie crumbs, cinnamon, coffee, and melted butter. Pat and press the mixture firmly over the bottom and 1½ inches up the side of the pan (use half the crumbs to cover the bottom, half for the side). Place pan in freezer while you mix the filling.

3.   Preheat the oven to 350 degrees.

4.   Melt both chocolates over warm water.

5.   Place cream cheese in the bowl of an electric mixer and cream

SERVES 10
INGREDIENTS
6 ounces semisweet chocolate, cut into pieces
2 ounces unsweetened chocolate, cut into pieces
16 ounces cream cheese, at room temperature
2 eggs
½ cup granulated sugar
½ teaspoon vanilla extract
1 tablespoon cocoa powder
1 teaspoon instant coffee powder
1½ cups sour cream
2 tablespoons unsalted butter, melted
Shavings or curls of semisweet chocolate

CRUST
1½ cups chocolate wafer cookie crumbs
Pinch cinnamon
½ teaspoon instant coffee powder
6 tablespoons unsalted butter, melted

it well. Turn off the mixer and add the eggs, sugar, vanilla, cocoa, and coffee. Beat until thoroughly mixed.

6.   With the mixer on low speed, add the melted chocolate, sour cream, and melted butter and continue beating until well blended. Scrape down the bowl at least once.

7.   Pour the mixture into the prepared crust and smooth the top. Place pan on a rimmed baking tray to catch any escaping butter. Bake for 45 minutes. Remove from oven and cool at room temperature. Cover and refrigerate for at least 6 hours before serving.

8.   To remove cheesecake from pan, run a knife around the edge of the form, then release the sides. Slide a long, heavy knife between the wax paper and pan bottom and ease off the cake. Peel off the wax

paper and place the cheesecake onto a flat serving platter. This dessert may be garnished with shaved or curled chocolate if you wish.

NOTE

For an alternate decoration, brush melted chocolate over an 8-inch circle drawn on wax paper. Chill, peel off paper, then center the round on top of the cheesecake. Place 2 sheets of paper over the top and leave a ½-inch opening between them. Sieve on some confectioners' sugar, then carefully lift and move papers to another spot. Continue sifting sugar and moving the papers until the top of the cake is criss-crossed with 5 or 6 white lines.

Chocolate Dropped Pie

INGREDIENTS

4 ounces unsweetened chocolate
4 ounces semisweet chocolate
6 tablespoons unsalted butter
4 eggs, at room temperature
1/2 cup tightly packed light brown sugar
3 tablespoons all-purpose flour
1/4 teaspoon salt
1/3 cup heavy cream
3 tablespoons dark rum
1 cup heavy cream
Confectioners' sugar
Vanilla extract
Large shavings of semisweet chocolate

A puffed chocolate shell that is literally dropped from a height so that it collapses into a dense fudge base, meant as an excuse on which to pile a mountain of whipped cream.

1. Preheat oven to 375 degrees. Butter a 10-inch springform pan.

2. Melt the chocolates and butter together over hot water.

3. Place eggs in a bowl of an electric mixer and beat at medium speed until frothy. Gradually add the brown sugar, then continue beating eggs for 8 minutes, or until they are thick and exceedingly pale in color.

4. Fold in the flour, melted chocolate, cream, and rum, and blend by hand until just mixed. Pour into the prepared baking pan and smooth the batter up the sides as much as possible. Bake for around 20 minutes, or until a toothpick inserted in the center comes out clean.

5. Place a kitchen towel on a counter. Hold the pie on both sides about 8 inches above the towel. Drop the pie down onto the surface. Immediately place 2 thicknesses of paper towels at the center of the pie and press down the center with the palms of your hands, but leave the outer rim intact. The pie will crack on the surface but that is all right.

6. Let the pie cool completely. Slide a knife around the edge of the pan, then release the side. Slide a thin spatula under the pie and slip the crust onto a serving dish.

7. Whip the cream, then flavor and sweeten to taste with sugar and vanilla. Heap in the center of the crust. Adorn the surface with chocolate shavings if you are so inclined.

Irish Coffee Pie

A light, cold, flavorful dessert that is especially good in hot weather.

1. Preheat oven to 350 degrees. Prepare the crust as directed in the cheesecake recipe (page 86). Pack the mixture into an ungreased 10-inch pie plate. Press greased aluminum foil over and into the crust, then fill foil with beans or other weights. Bake for 15 minutes, remove beans and foil, and bake for another 5 minutes. Remove from oven and let cool.

2. To prepare the filling, scald the milk. In a medium saucepan, place yolks, cocoa, coffee, and suga and stir until blended. Dissolve gelatin in the whiskey.

3. Slowly pour the hot milk into the egg yolks, stirring all the while. Place saucepan over low heat and stir until the custard thickens.

SERVES 8 TO 10

INGREDIENTS

1 Chocolate Mocha Cheesecake crust (page 86)
2 cups milk
6 egg yolks
2 tablespoons cocoa powder
2 tablespoons instant coffee powder
⅔ cup granulated sugar
2 envelopes unflavored gelatin
6 tablespoons Irish whiskey
1 cup heavy cream
Whipped cream
Chocolate curls or shavings

(Do not allow to simmer.) Off the heat, add the gelatin and stir until it dissolves. Strain the mixture through a sieve.

4. Let the custard cool in the refrigerator, but keep a close eye on it and stir it frequently. When it threatens to set, quickly whip the heavy cream to soft peaks and fold it thoroughly into the custard. Pour the mixture into the baked pie shell and put pie to chill.

5. Just before serving, garnish pie with rosettes of whipped cream and chocolate curls.

Black Bottom Pie

There are many varieties of Black Bottom Pie. This one has a very dense chocolate bottom, indeed.

1. Preheat the oven to 350 degrees.

2. To make the crust, combine wafer crumbs, butter, ginger, and vanilla. Mix with your fingertips until blended, then press into a 9-inch pie dish. Bake for 8 to 10 minutes or until the crust is lightly golden. Remove from oven and immediately scatter the grated chocolate over the bottom of the shell. Smooth with the back of a spoon and leave to cool.

3. To make the filling, soften the gelatin in the water and set aside. Beat the egg yolks until very thick. Add ½ cup of the sugar, the cornstarch, and the salt.

4. Place the half 'n half and chocolate in a small pan and stir until the chocolate melts. Pour the

SERVES 8

CRUST

1½ cups vanilla wafer crumbs
4 tablespoons unsalted butter, softened
¼ teaspoon ginger
1 teaspoon vanilla extract
3 ounces semisweet chocolate, finely grated

INGREDIENTS

1 tablespoon unflavored gelatin
¼ cup cold water
2 whole eggs plus 2 yolks
¾ cup granulated sugar
1 tablespoon cornstarch
Pinch salt
1½ cups half 'n half
2 ounces unsweetened chocolate
1½ cups heavy cream
2 tablespoons light or dark rum
Whipped cream and chocolate shavings for garnish

hot milk slowly into the egg yolk mixture. Return the mixture to the heat and whisk until smooth and medium thick. Off the heat, add the gelatin and stir until it dissolves into the custard. Cover and place in refrigerator until the gelatin just begins to set.

5. Whip the cream. Beat the egg whites until they begin to thicken, then slowly add the remaining ¼ cup of sugar and continue beating until thick and glossy but not stiff. Gently stir the custard and half the cream together and then fold in the beaten whites. Pour the mixture into the crust and refrigerate until firm. Top with the remaining whipped cream and chocolate shavings.

Chocolate Pecan Pie

A rich but light-textured pie that is full of nuts and chocolate.

1. To prepare the crust, mix the flour and salt in a bowl. Cut in the butter until it is well blended and the mixture looks like fine oatmeal. Sprinkle on the water, draw the dough together into a ball, then give the dough 2 or 3 kneads to ensure smoothness. Cover with plastic wrap and refrigerate for 30 minutes.

2. Preheat the oven to 350 degrees.

3. Roll out the dough and fit it into a 10-inch pie dish. Line the dough with foil, then pour in dried beans and bake the crust blind for 10 minutes. Remove beans and foil and let crust cook another 5 minutes. Remove from oven.

4. To make the filling, cream the butter and sugar until very light.

SERVES 8 TO 10

CRUST
1¼ cups all-purpose flour
¼ teaspoon salt
6 tablespoons unsalted butter, chilled and cut in small chunks
⅓ cup ice water

INGREDIENTS
1 stick unsalted butter
⅔ cup tightly packed light brown sugar
3 eggs
¼ teaspoon salt
1 teaspoon vanilla extract
1 tablespoon bourbon
½ cup corn syrup
3 tablespoons molasses
1 heaping tablespoon flour
1⅓ cups shelled pecans, chopped
½ cup semisweet chocolate chips
Stiffly whipped cream, sweetened to taste and flavored with vanilla or bourbon

Add the eggs, 1 at a time, and stir well after each addition. Add salt, vanilla, bourbon, corn syrup, and molasses, and blend well.

5. Sprinkle the flour over the nuts, then add nuts and chocolate to the filling and pour into the pie shell. Bake for 35 minutes or until a knife inserted in the pie's center comes out with no damp crumbs on it. Protect the surface of the pie with foil if it threatens to overbrown.

6. Let the pie cool to room temperature, then serve portions with generous mounds of whipped cream.

Chocolate Orange Chess Tart

SERVES 10

A crisp, thin dark crust holds a thin orange chess filling, a layer of bittersweet chocolate glazes the top. When the tart is cut it shows a striking and sophisticated stratification.

INGREDIENTS

Zest of 2 oranges (preferably Temple oranges), finely grated
1²/₃ cups granulated sugar
1 stick unsalted butter, at room temperature
5 eggs (medium or large)
2 tablespoons all-purpose flour
1 tablespoon corn meal
¹/₂ cup freshly squeezed orange juice
3 ounces bittersweet chocolate (preferably Tobler Extra-Bittersweet), very finely grated
2 small seedless oranges, thinly sliced
Thickly whipped cream

CRUST

1¹/₂ cups fine chocolate wafer cookie crumbs
6 tablespoons unsalted butter, melted

1. Cut a circle of wax paper to fit the bottom of an 11-inch springform pan. Butter the paper and the sides of the pan.

2. To make the crust, mix crumbs and melted butter. Pat and press the mixture firmly over the bottom and 1 inch up the sides of the pan. Place pan in freezer while mixing the filling.

3. Preheat the oven to 350 degrees.

4. To make the filling, combine orange zest and sugar. Work the mixture between your fingertips until the sugar is well impregnated with the orange essence.

5. With an electric mixer, cream the butter. Gradually add the sugar, then beat in the eggs 1 at a time. Add flour, corn meal, and orange juice.

6. Place mixture in the top of a double boiler (if you are hesitant about making custards) or in a heavy saucepan directly over low heat. Stir the mixture constantly. It will first loosen as the butter melts, then gradually thicken as the eggs begin to heat. Under no account must the mixture come near a simmer. The final texture should be that of a medium-thick crème anglaise or cream sauce.

7. Pour the mixture into the prepared pie shell. Place the baking dish on a cookie sheet and bake for 25 to 30 minutes, or until the top is completely firm and just beginning to brown. Turn the pie in the oven if it threatens to bake unevenly.

8. When the pie comes from the oven, sprinkle on the grated chocolate and it will melt into a smooth glaze. Use a spatula to smooth the surface. Let the tart cool completely.

9. Release the springform side and lift out the tart. Slide a spatula under the pie and you should be able to transfer it to a platter and peel off the wax paper in 1 step.

10. Cut the garnishing orange slices two-thirds of the way through and give each slice a half twist. Rim the tart with fresh orange slices and pipe small rosettes of cream along the border. Serve at room temperature or just slightly chilled.

Chocolate Truffle Cakes

Here are some very grown-up chocolate cream-filled cupcakes indeed!

1. Preheat oven to 375 degrees. Butter and flour six 4-inch (1½-cup) soufflé dishes. (You could also use 3 large cupcake tins for more and smaller cakes.) Cut rounds of parchment paper and place them at the bottom of each mold. Butter the paper.

2. Place egg yolks and half the sugar in the bowl of an electric mixer and beat for 8 minutes, or until the eggs are thick and pale.

3. Sift together the flour, cocoa, baking powder, and salt.

4. Start beating the egg whites and when they are fluffy, slowly add the remaining sugar and continue beating until they form stiff peaks.

5. Fold the flour and butter alternately into the yolk mixture.

SERVES 6 TO 8

INGREDIENTS

3 ounces bittersweet
  chocolate
Cocoa powder
Rum, Grand Marnier, or
  amaretto liqueur
½ cup heavy cream, well
  chilled
Confectioners' sugar
1 recipe Nouvelle Chocolat
  Sauce (page 170)
½ cup sliced almonds,
  lightly toasted, then
  broken into small pieces

CAKE BATTER

5 eggs, separated and at
  room temperature
⅓ cup granulated sugar
⅓ cup sifted all-purpose
  flour
¼ cup cocoa powder
1 teaspoon baking powder
Pinch salt
3 tablespoons unsalted
  butter, melted

Add a large scoop of the whites and fold and stir until the chocolate base is well blended. Fold in the remaining whites gently.

6. Divide the batter among the buttered molds. Set the molds on a baking sheet and place in oven. Bake for 18 to 20 minutes, or until a cake tester comes out clean. Remove from oven, let cakes sit 5 minutes, then turn out onto a cooling rack, rounded side up. Let cool completely.

7. Melt the chocolate over hot water. Set aside.

8. Trim the cakes slightly at the edges to round them. Brush the tops and sides of the cakes with melted chocolate. Let chocolate harden briefly, then roll cakes lightly in cocoa to get the look of a candy truffle.

9. Dig out a large tuft of the inside crumb from the bottom of

each cake. Generously sprinkle the interior of each cake with the liquor of your choice.

10. Thirty minutes before serving, whip the cream stiff and flavor it with confectioners' sugar and more of the same liquor as before. Fit a pastry bag with a small rosette tube, and pipe the cream into the bottom of each cake.

11. Set the cakes on individual serving dishes. Pipe a small rosette of cream atop each.

12. Prepare the Nouvelle Chocolate Sauce to be of easy floating consistency. Stir in the almonds, then spoon the crunchy sauce around the bottom of each cake so that it floats to the rim of the plate. Trace a spiral of chocolate sauce on top.

Chocolate-Dipped Profiteroles

In this version, profiteroles are dipped in melted chocolate and topped with cream.

1. Preheat oven to 350 degrees. Grease or oil a baking sheet.

2. Place water, butter, salt, and sugar in a saucepan. Let the butter melt over medium heat, then turn up heat and let the liquid come to a fierce boil. Remove from heat and immediately pour in all the flour at once. Stir with a heavy spoon, then return mixture to a lowered heat and continue stirring rapidly for around 2 minutes or until the mixture is very dry and begins to cake slightly on the bottom of the pan. Remove from heat and let sit for a minute.

3. Add and stir in 1 whole egg at a time. Stir in the egg white. The paste should be smooth before each egg is added. Stir in vanilla.

AROUND 2 DOZEN SMALL PASTRIES

INGREDIENTS

1 cup water
1 stick unsalted butter
1/4 teaspoon salt
1 teaspoon granulated sugar
1 cup sifted all-purpose flour
4 whole eggs, plus 1 egg, separated
1/4 teaspoon vanilla extract
6 ounces semisweet or bittersweet chocolate
2/3 cup heavy cream, whipped stiff and sweetened and flavored to taste

4. Scoop the paste into a pastry bag fitted with a large plain tube. Press out small, egg-sized portions of dough. Beat the remaining egg yolk with 1 teaspoon of water, then brush the egg yolk glaze over the surface of each portion.

5. Bake for 12 minutes. Pull tray from oven, puncture the bottom of each pastry with a knife, then return pastries to oven for another 3 minutes to dry. Remove and cool.

6. Melt the chocolate over hot water. Keep warm.

7. Fit a pastry bag with a small star tube. Fill the bag with whipped cream and press cream into the bottom of each pastry until it fills the hollow interior of the puff. Quickly dip the pastry top in the melted chocolate, then place on a tray, chocolate side up, and let harden in the refrigerator. Top each puff with a rosette of whipped cream.

Crisp Downside Upcakes

These are plump rounded cakes that have been baked in a pool of caramel. Turn them out upside down and the nut and caramel topping will become chewy crisp.

1. Preheat oven to 350 degrees. With a buttered finger, lightly grease only the sides of 18 cupcake tins.

2. For the topping, place butter, corn syrup, and water in a small saucepan. Warm over low heat just until the butter melts, then stir in the brown sugar. Spoon a scant tablespoon portion of the mixture into each cupcake mold. Top each with a few pecan pieces, about 4 bits to a cake.

3. Melt the chocolates for the batter. Set aside.

4. Cream together the butter and sugars until light and fluffy. Add

YIELDS 18
INGREDIENTS
2 ounces semisweet
  chocolate
1 ounce unsweetened
  chocolate
1/3 cup unsalted butter
1/2 cup granulated sugar
1/2 cup tightly packed light
  brown sugar
2 eggs, lightly beaten
1 1/3 cups sifted all-purpose
  flour
1 tablespoon cocoa powder
2 teaspoons baking powder
1/4 teaspoon salt
1/2 cup milk

TOPPING
5 tablespoons unsalted
  butter
3 tablespoons corn syrup
2 tablespoons water
1/2 cup tightly packed light
  brown sugar
1 cup shelled whole pecans,
  small ones left whole,
  larger ones broken in half

the eggs and continue beating until the mixture is thick and smooth. Add the melted chocolate.

5. Sift together the flour, cocoa, baking powder, and salt. Add the dry ingredients to the batter alternating with the milk.

6. Spoon batter into the cupcake pans. It will seem rather scant. Bake for 20 minutes, or until the caramel has turned a good amber color. (You will see it bubbling around cakes.) Remove from oven and turn out at once so that the hot caramel can drip down the sides of the cakes. Cool cakes to let them crisp. Serve with lightly sweetened whipped cream.

Chocolate Gâteau de Plomb

SERVES 16

INGREDIENTS

6 egg yolks
²/₃ cup granulated sugar
½ cup heavy cream
2 ounces unsalted butter, melted
Generous ¼ teaspoon salt
2 teaspoons vanilla extract
Zest of 1 lemon, finely grated
4 cups all-purpose flour (approximately), sifted after *measuring*
8 ounces miniature semisweet chocolate chips or *squares semi-sweet chocolate, well chopped*
½ cup confectioners' sugar

*H*ere is an updated version of a recipe from Antonin Carême, the famous late 18th-century French chef to Talleyrand and Czar Alexander, among others. This large plomb (lead) pastry, a traditional fête des rois *sweet*, is one of the earliest uses of chocolate in cooking I have found. Carême says to bake this pastry in an oven for 2½ hours, but in our day, a 40-minute bake produces a crisp rustic pastry.

1. Place egg yolks, sugar, cream, butter, salt, vanilla, and lemon zest in a bowl and stir until well blended. Add in the flour by cupfuls until you can turn out the dough onto a floured board. Continue working in the flour and mixing gently with your hands until the dough is firm enough to roll out with a pin. Place ⅕ of the dough in plastic wrap, and put in the freezer.

2. Lightly grease the *back* of a baking sheet or pizza pan. Place the dough on the pan and roll out a circle roughly 10½ inches in diameter. Spread chocolate chips over surface to within ½ inch of the edge.

3. On a floured surface, roll out the remaining portion of dough from the freezer. When it is very thin and as large as the bottom piece, place it over the top of the chocolate and press together both free edges of the dough so that the chocolate is entirely enclosed. (Pinch together any small splits that may open on the top.) Press a decorative border around the edge of the pastry with your fingertips. Sieve confectioners' sugar over top. Let pastry sit while you preheat the oven to 325 degrees.

4. Bake for 40 minutes. Remove from oven, let cool briefly, then slide the pastry off the pan and onto cooling rack. Let cool before cutting into wedges. This dessert is best served very fresh.

Chocolate Linzer Tart

A variation on a classic theme, with chocolate added to the already pleasing combination of almonds and raspberries. This large cookie/tart is delicious served along with a fruit compote or homemade vanilla ice cream.

1. Place ground almonds, cookie crumbs, flour, sugar, cinnamon, and cocoa in a large bowl and mix well. Distribute the butter over the mixture and add the egg yolks. Work the dough with your fingertips, rubbing in the butter and finally amalgamating the ingredients into a smooth dough. Wrap the dough in plastic wrap and refrigerate for 30 minutes before rolling.

2. Preheat the oven to 350 degrees.

3. Lightly butter an 11½-inch pizza pan with sides. (Or you may

SERVES 12 TO 15

INGREDIENTS

1½ cups ground blanched almonds, plus 2 tablespoons finely chopped almonds for garnishing
1⅓ cups chocolate wafer cookie crumbs (such as Nabisco's Famous Chocolate Wafers)
1 cup sifted all-purpose flour
¾ cup granulated sugar
¼ teaspoon ground cinnamon
2 tablespoons cocoa powder
2 sticks unsalted butter, cut into bits
2 egg yolks
1 cup raspberry jam
Cocoa powder

make 2 smaller tarts in 8-inch round pans, but the pans must have sides.) Use ¾ of the dough to line the bottom of the pan and 1½ inches up the sides. The dough is most easily rolled with a glass tumbler and pressed into the pan with your fingers.

4. Spread the jam thickly over the crust but not quite to the edges.

5. Press a decorative border of dough around the edge of the crust with your thumb. Roll the remaining dough out thinly on a cocoa-covered surface and cut out small circles, half-circles, or hearts. Pattern them over the jam. Sprinkle on chopped almonds.

6. Bake for 35 minutes. Let the pastry cool in the pan, then cut into neat wedges.

Chocolate Coconut Bars

A good, rapidly assembled cookie bar topped with nuts, coconut, and chocolate. These keep fresh and moist for many days.

1. Preheat oven to 325 degrees. Butter an 8 by 12-inch baking pan.

2. To prepare the crust, cream together the butter and brown sugar. When it is light and fluffy, stir in salt, flour, and cocoa. Spread and press the dough lightly into the prepared baking pan. Bake for 15 minutes.

3. While the crust is baking, prepare the topping. Beat the eggs with an electric mixer until frothy. Add brown sugar, vanilla, flour, and baking powder. Blend well. Stir in the coconut, pecans, and half the chocolate chips.

4. When the crust has baked for 15 minutes, remove it from the oven and spread the topping over it. Scatter the remaining chocolate chips over the top. Bake for another 25 minutes.

5. Cool the pastry on a rack, then cut into thin strips.

YIELDS 30 BARS
INGREDIENTS

2 eggs
1 cup tightly packed light
    brown sugar
1 teaspoon vanilla extract
2 tablespoons all-purpose
    flour
1/2 teaspoon baking powder
1 1/4 cups shredded coconut
2/3 cup shelled pecans,
    chopped
1 cup semisweet chocolate
    chips

CRUST

1 stick unsalted butter,
    softened
1 1/2 cups tightly packed
    light brown sugar
1/2 teaspoon salt
1 cup minus 2 tablespoons
    sifted all-purpose flour
1/4 cup cocoa powder

Three-layered Chocolate Almond Bars

*P*at a base of short crust into a baking dish, cover it with melted chocolate and nuts, then top it all with a crunch of almond meringue. When cut into squares, you have this tasty bar cookie.

1. Preheat the oven to 350 degrees.

2. To make the short crust, mix flour, sugar, and salt in a bowl. Add the butter and work it into the flour with your fingertips until the mixture becomes flaky. Sprinkle with a bit of water and, working the dough as little as possible, pack the mixture into a ball.

3. Roll the dough out onto a lightly floured surface. The entire amount will be used to fill a 13 × 9 baking pan, so when it is large enough to cover the pan's surface, transfer the dough to the dish and press it over the bottom and about 1

YIELDS 12 BARS
INGREDIENTS

1 cup sifted all-purpose flour
2 tablespoons confectioners' sugar
Pinch salt
6 tablespoons unsalted butter, chilled and cut in bits
1 or 2 tablespoons water
⅓ cup semisweet chocolate chips

CHOCOLATE LAYER

1 cup semisweet chocolate chips
2 tablespoons butter
Pinch salt
½ cup ground almonds
1 egg plus 1 egg yolk
1 teaspoon vanilla extract

MERINGUE

1 egg white
¾ cup ground almonds
1½ cups confectioners' sugar

inch up the sides. Trim the sides evenly.

4. To make the chocolate layer, melt the chips over hot water. Cool briefly, then stir in butter, salt, almonds, egg and yolk, and finally the vanilla. Immediately smooth the mixture over the short crust.

5. To make the meringue, lightly beat the egg white to a froth. Mix together the almonds and sugar, then stir in the egg white. Smooth the thick mixture over the chocolate. Fold over the short crust on the sides slightly to completely encase the chocolate.

6. Bake for 45 minutes. Remove pan from oven and let cool completely.

7. Melt the chocolate chips over hot water and drizzle small threads of the chocolate back and forth across the top of the pastry. Cut in squares and serve.

Six-Layer Chocolate Cookie Bars

Six different layers of crisp crumbs, melting candy chips, nuts, and coconut combine to build these delicious, rapidly made cookie bars.

1. Preheat oven to 350 degrees. Lightly butter a 9 by 13-inch baking pan.

2. Mix graham cracker crumbs and melted butter until the crumbs are moist and of an even, small texture. Pat the crumbs into the bottom of the buttered baking pan.

3. Scatter chocolate chips over the crumb crust. Scatter butterscotch chips over chocolate. Sprinkle on the pecans. Layer the coconut evenly over the surface. Drizzle the condensed milk over the entire surface.

4. Bake for 25 to 30 minutes. The coconut should turn a handsome golden brown.

YIELDS 24 BARS

INGREDIENTS

1 cup graham cracker crumbs
3/4 cup unsalted butter, melted
1 cup semisweet chocolate chips
1 cup butterscotch chips
1 cup chopped pecans
1 cup shredded coconut
1 can (14 ounces) sweetened condensed milk

5. Let cookie bars cool in the baking dish, then cut them into small bars and remove to serving platter.

Chocolate Cabbage Cake, page 62

High Protein Chocolate Crunch Bars

*O*ne way to ensure a healthy dessert or lunchbox sweet is to make these protein rich bars.

1. Butter a 9 by 9-inch baking pan.

2. Combine the syrup and brown sugar in a saucepan. Bring to a boil over medium heat, stirring all the while. Remove from heat and immediately stir in the peanut butter and butter. Oil your hands, then quickly stir and blend syrup and cereal together. Scrape mixture into the baking pan and press down on the mixture to compact it somewhat.

3. Combine the chocolate and butterscotch chips in a pan and let them melt over hot water. Drizzle the melted chocolate over the cereal mixture. Let stand until completely cool and firm, then cut into small bars.

YIELDS 16 SMALL SQUARES

INGREDIENTS

¾ *cup light corn syrup*
¾ *cup packed light brown sugar*
1 *cup crunchy peanut butter*
1 *teaspoon unsalted butter*
5 *cups high protein cereal*
¾ *cup semisweet chocolate chips*
¼ *cup butterscotch chips*

Frozen Cassata Torte, page 166

Chocolate Shortbread

Intensely chocolate and not too sweet, this shortbread makes a splendid present. I like to eat it with sweet, ripe pears.

1. Preheat the oven to 350 degrees.

2. Melt chocolate over hot water and cool slightly.

3. Cream the butter and sugar together, then add chocolate and blend well.

4. Sift the cocoa, flour, and cornstarch over the butter mixture and, using your fingertips, blend in lightly. The secret of successful shortbread is in the blending; work only until the mixture lightly crumbles—when if you press down, you could compact the mixture easily.

5. This amount of dough fills a 9-inch shortbread mold or a round cake pan. Scatter 1 tablespoon of

SERVES 8

INGREDIENTS

1 ounce unsweetened chocolate
1 stick unsalted butter
²/₃ cup confectioners' sugar, sifted after *measuring*
2 tablespoons cocoa powder
1¹/₄ cups sifted all-purpose flour
1 tablespoon cornstarch or rice flour
Granulated sugar for mold

granulated sugar in mold. Put the dough into the mold and gently press down until the surface is smooth and firm.

6. Lightly grease a baking sheet. Stand the mold up on end at the center of the sheet and push over. Remove the mold to have a perfectly formed round. If not, reform the dough in the mold again. The traditional shortbread mold, with its sun-ray border, is a relic of pagan sun worship. You can, if you wish, run the flat side of a knife around the edge of a plain round to simulate the design, and you should lightly score the round into 8 divisions so cookie will divide neatly after baking.

7. Bake for 25 minutes. Cover lightly with aluminum foil for the last 10 minutes of baking. The shortbread will feel soft when it is taken from the oven. Let cool until firm enough to transfer to a cake rack.

Saucepan Brownies

A nice cakelike brownie that only uses 1 pan in the preparation. This is good for meeting bake sale or quick after-school obligations.

1.   Preheat oven to 350 degrees. Grease a 9 by 13-inch pan.

2.   In a heavy, medium-sized saucepan, melt the butter and chocolates over very low heat, stirring occasionally. When all are melted, remove from heat and stir in sugars and vanilla. Add flour, salt, and baking powder, and mix well. Then add the eggs, stirring briefly after each addition. Stir in nuts, if desired.

3.   Bake brownies for 25 to 30 minutes, or until a toothpick inserted at the center comes out dry. Cool, then cut into squares. This brownie needs no frosting.

YIELDS 24

INGREDIENTS

1 stick plus 3 tablespoons unsalted butter
2 ounces semisweet chocolate
4 ounces unsweetened chocolate
1 cup tightly packed light brown sugar
1 cup granulated sugar
1 1/2 teaspoons vanilla extract
1 1/3 cups sifted all-purpose flour
1 teaspoon salt
2 teaspoons baking powder
4 eggs
1/2 cup chopped nuts of choice (optional)

Designer Brownies

A status brownie, this is so good that it deserves its own initials. Frost these brownies with light Cocoa Frosting, then pipe on your own stylized signature markings with dark bittersweet chocolate.

1. Preheat oven to 375 degrees. Butter and flour a 9 by 13-inch baking pan.

2. Melt the chocolate and butter together over hot water. Stir to blend, then put aside to cool slightly. Stir in coffee, cinnamon, and vanilla.

3. Place eggs and salt in the bowl of an electric mixer and beat until slightly thickened. Add the sugar slowly, in 5 or 6 portions, and continue beating the eggs for 10 minutes. The consistency should be perfectly smooth. (Feel the eggs with your fingers; there should be no undissolved granules of sugar.)

INGREDIENTS

*6 ounces unsweetened
    chocolate
1 1/2 sticks unsalted butter
1 tablespoon instant coffee
    powder
1/4 teaspoon ground
    cinnamon
1 tablespoon vanilla
    extract
4 eggs
1/4 teaspoon salt
2 1/3 cups granulated sugar
1 1/4 cups all-purpose flour,
    sifted after measuring*

When the mixer is lifted up, the eggs that drop from it should remain in a firm pattern on the surface for a full 30 seconds.

4. Stir in the chocolate until just blended, then fold in the flour, lifting and turning the mass only until the flour is fully incorporated.

5. Pour the batter into the prepared pan and smooth the top. Bake for 15 minutes, then cover the brownies lightly with a sheet of aluminum foil and continue baking for another 20 minutes.

6. Remove from oven and place pan on a cake rack. Remove foil and let the brownies sit for 2 hours before frosting.

7. For the frosting, melt the butter in a saucepan and let it turn just slightly nut-brown. Remove pan from the heat and add the vanilla, cocoa, food coloring, egg, and sugar.

Beat with an electric mixer or whisk until very smooth. Spread the frosting over the brownies and let it harden. For a professional look, the brownies should be marked off with a ruler before cutting to ensure even lines.

8.   To add a designer logo, melt the chocolate over hot water and then let it cool slightly. Make a small paper piping bag (see page xviii), and fill it with chocolate. Snip off a small point with scissors and squeeze out chocolate to initial the brownies. If, for instance, your name is Linda Vickers, you may want to draw an *L,* then add a *V* to its lower line. Place a small cross at each corner. Let the markings be neat and precise, as if stamped on.

COCOA FROSTING

*3 tablespoons unsalted
  butter*
¹/₂ teaspoon vanilla extract
1 tablespoon cocoa powder
2 drops red food coloring
1 egg
*1 cup confectioners' sugar
  (approximately), sifted
  after measuring*
*3 ounces bittersweet
  chocolate for initials*

Schokoladekartöffelchen

This is a clever Austrian trompe l'oeil *confection which translates as "cocoa potatoes." It consists of delectable sponge biscuits encased in almond paste, then lightly rolled in cocoa. Press in some realistic "eyes" with a skewer, then mound the pastries in a wooden vegetable basket purloined from a produce market.*

1. Preheat the oven to 375 degrees. Cover a baking sheet with parchment paper. Fit a pastry bag with a plain ½-inch nozzle.

2. Make a simple syrup by combining the sugar and water. Bring to a slow boil and cook for 5 minutes. Let cool, then add the rum. Set aside.

3. To make the pastry, beat the egg yolks, ⅓ cup of sugar, and vanilla together until thick and white. Beat the whites until they be-

YIELDS 12

INGREDIENTS

4 ounces bittersweet
  chocolate, or ½ cup
  raspberry jam
10 ounces almond paste
Confectioners' sugar
Cocoa powder
Slivered almonds

SYRUP

¾ cup granulated sugar
¾ cup water
2 tablespoons light rum

PASTRY

3 eggs, separated and at
  room temperature
⅓ cup granulated sugar,
  plus 1 tablespoon for
  whites
1 teaspoon vanilla extract
⅔ cup sifted all-purpose
  flour

gin to thicken and stiffen, then slowly add remaining sugar and continue beating until the whites are stiff, glossy, but still moist (do not overbeat to a dry, collapsing foam).

4. Add the flour and ⅓ of the whites to the yolks and stir together. When just blended, add the remaining whites and fold gently into the batter.

5. Transfer the batter to the pastry bag. (Place bag in a small bowl and fold up the tube end so no batter escapes.) Pipe a small dot of batter under each corner of the paper so the parchment will not slip. Pipe 24 egg-shaped ovals, about 2½ inches long and 1¼ inches wide, directly onto the paper.

6. Turn the oven down to 350 degrees and place in the baking tray. Bake for around 15 minutes. The pastries should be a rich golden color. Remove from the oven, peel

them off the paper, and immediately dip each into the rum syrup.

7.   Sandwich the flat sides of 2 pastries together with either melted chocolate or raspberry jam. If using chocolate, refrigerate the pastries briefly to harden the chocolate before going on to the next step.

8.   Sieve a light dusting of confectioners' sugar onto a counter or pastry marble. Break off a portion of almond paste and roll it out on the sugar-covered counter until it is close to paper thin. (I can see my table's marble markings through the paste.) Sieve more sugar on top as necessary to ease the rolling process.

9.   Cut off a portion of almond paste large enough to envelop one of the pastries, and wrap it around the cookie, coaxing and forming the almond covering all the while until the object resembles a potato. Re-

move all excess almond paste; there should be only the thinnest of coverings.

10.   Use a skewer or nail to make indentions here and there in the skin, then roll the potatoes in cocoa and smooth it over the surface with your fingers. Knock off excess, and stick 3 or 4 small almond slivers into each potato to simulate eyes.

Chocolate Honeycombs

Handsome and unusual choco-late pastries, these crisp rounds would be good accompaniments to a chilled compote of oranges. Place them whole on the table and let guests simply break off portions. These are best prepared in cool dry weather. Note: a nonstick pan is an absolute must.

1. Preheat oven to 340 degrees. To make the pastries, choose a frying pan that can be transferred to the oven. Butter the frying pan generously.

2. Combine in a bowl the almonds, sugar, flour, cocoa, and cinnamon.

3. Place the butter and milk in a small saucepan. Let the butter melt over low heat. Stir in the dry ingredients, then turn up the heat to medium and let the mixture come to a lightly bubbling simmer around the

SERVES 12

INGREDIENTS

1 cup finely ground
  almonds
1/3 cup plus 1 tablespoon
  granulated sugar
2 tablespoons all-purpose
  flour
2 teaspoons cocoa powder
1/4 teaspoon ground
  cinnamon
1 stick unsalted butter
2 tablespoons milk
4 ounces semisweet
  chocolate

edges of the pan. Stir constantly. Remove pan from heat as soon as the simmer is reached.

4. Heat the frying pan until the butter coating has just melted and the pan is warm. Spoon in half the batter and smooth it as neatly as possible. Place the pan in the hot oven and let bake for around 10 minutes. Watch carefully after 8 minutes, as the mixture goes through a caramelizing process. Turn the pan if heat is too intense at one side of the oven. The entire surface of the pastry should be covered with broken bubbles; the edge of the pastry will look feathery. The color should be a rich, light cocoa, just turning a slightly darker amber at the edge. Don't let the edge overbrown.

5. Remove pan from the oven and let cool briefly on a cake rack. Keep testing the edge of the pastry with a spatula. As the pastry cools,

start under the edge and keep releasing the pastry with firm scrapes of the spatula. The entire circumference will loosen first, and finally the center. Lift out the crisp round, and let it cool completely.

6.   Clean out the pan and repeat the process to cook the remaining pastry. Gently reheat the batter before proceeding.

7.   When pastries are cool, melt semisweet chocolate and brush chocolate over their tops. If not to be eaten soon, cover and store pastries in an airtight container to keep them fresh.

Candied Orange and Ginger Florentines

A fragile but deliciously sophisticated florentine without the usual candied cherries.

1. To make the candied orange, cut the zest (the outer orange coloring only, with no white pith attached) off the orange in long strips. Cut the strips into ⅛-inch-wide julienne, then cut into ½-inch lengths. Place orange strips, sugar, and water in a small saucepan. Let simmer over very low heat until the bottom of the pan is covered only with glazed strips of orange. Do not allow to caramelize. Remove orange and discard any extra syrup.

2. Preheat oven to 350 degrees. Butter and flour 2 cookie sheets.

3. Melt the butter in a saucepan. Add the sugar, stir briefly, then place over medium heat and bring to a full boil. Immediately remove

YIELDS 12 TO 15

INGREDIENTS

6 tablespoons unsalted butter
⅓ cup granulated sugar
1 heaping tablespoon minced crystallized ginger
½ cup sliced almonds
2 tablespoons heavy cream
6 ounces bittersweet chocolate, chopped

CANDIED ORANGE

1 large or 2 small navel oranges
¼ cup granulated sugar
½ cup water

the pan from the heat and stir in candied orange zest, ginger, almonds, and cream. Stir until slightly thick and creamy looking.

4. Place 6 separate tablespoons of the mixture far apart on each baking tray—the pastries will spread enormously. Flatten down the mixture as much as possible. Bake for 6 minutes, or until the liquid has turned to a handsome caramel. Remove from oven and immediately use a 2½- or 3-inch round cookie cutter to pull in any lopsided edges of the pastries so they are as uniformly round as possible. When they have firmed enough to cohere, lift off the cookies with a spatula and let them cool until completely hard.

5. Melt the chocolate over hot water. Set aside.

6. Place a layer of wax or parchment paper on a cookie sheet. When the chocolate is slightly cool,

spread a layer of chocolate ¼ inch thick over the paper, and immediately place the pastries on the chocolate. Refrigerate briefly, then use the cookie cutter to cut around the chocolate-covered florentines.

7. When the first coating of chocolate is cool, remelt the unused portions of chocolate. You may, if you wish, spread on another coating of chocolate, then draw the jagged edge of a pastry comb or butter scraper back and forth across the chocolate to imprint a handsome, professional pattern. Store in an airtight container in a cool place.

Chocolate Ladyfingers

*T*his is a useful recipe for ladyfingers, which can be used to line charlotte molds and soufflé dishes before mousses, bavarians, or trifles are poured in or layered. These can be trimmed to size with scissors and cut into a pattern when necessary. Ladyfingers will cooperate most when baked on a dry day.

1. Preheat oven to 350 degrees. Butter and flour a large cookie sheet. Fit a large 16-inch pastry bag with a ½-inch-wide plain tube. Twist the end of the bag and stuff it up into the tube; this will prevent the batter from coming out when the bag is filled.

2. In the bowl of an electric mixer, beat the egg yolks, ⅓ cup sugar, and vanilla to an especially thick ribbon. (When the batter is lifted and allowed to fall back, it should maintain a firm pattern for a good 10 seconds.)

YIELDS 24

INGREDIENTS

5 eggs, separated
⅔ cup granulated sugar
1 teaspoon vanilla extract
1 cup all-purpose flour,
*   sifted after measuring*
4 tablespoons cocoa
*   powder*
½ teaspoon ground
*   cinnamon*
Confectioners' sugar

3. Sift flour, cocoa, and cinnamon together. Add to the yolks 1 tablespoon at a time with the machine continuously beating at a low speed. The mixture will be exceedingly thick. Keep bowl on the machine on lowest speed.

4. In a separate bowl, beat the egg whites until they start to stiffen. Gradually sprinkle on the remaining sugar and beat until the peaks are firm and glossy, but do not allow them to overdry.

5. Spoon a quarter of the whites into the yolk mixture and let the machine slowly blend them in. Remove bowl from machine and fold in the remaining whites by hand.

6. Place all the batter into the pastry bag. Pipe out lengths of batter about 2½ to 3 inches long, as desired. (If you are going to use ladyfingers for a charlotte, pipe batter to

equal height of mold.) Leave room for expansion between each pastry, for they can expand to a good 1½ inches in width.

7. Sieve confectioners' sugar generously over the tops of the ladyfingers and place in oven for 20 minutes. When done, a tester inserted in a fat finger should come out clean. Let cool briefly; remove from sheet. Allow to cool and then serve or use for another dessert.

Chocolate Meringues

*C*risp and frothy, this mixture piped out as 2 large circles can form the basis for many possible desserts. It can, of course, also be piped into a variety of small forms, assembled into a formal vacherin, or made into bases for ice cream sundaes.

1. Preheat the oven to 300 degrees. Cut a piece of parchment paper or brown paper sacking to fit a large cookie sheet. Trace 2 10-inch circles on the paper.

2. Sift together the confectioners' sugar, cornstarch, and cocoa.

3. Beat the egg whites by hand in a large copper bowl, or use a mixer with a large bowl. When the whites form soft peaks, start slowly adding the granulated sugar, and continue to beat the whites until they form shiny, firm peaks.

**YIELDS 2
10-INCH CIRCLES**

INGREDIENTS

1 cup confectioners' sugar
1 tablespoon cornstarch
4 tablespoons cocoa
  powder
½ cup egg whites (about 5
  eggs)
½ cup granulated sugar

4. If you are using a mixer, reduce the speed to low and add the cocoa mixture 1 tablespoon at a time, and beat just until blended. If you are beating the whites by hand, fold the cocoa mixture into the whites in 4 batches.

5. Place a dab of meringue under each corner of the paper so it will hold in place on the cookie sheet. Place half the meringue in each circle and spread it evenly with a spatula until it fills the circle neatly. Leave the top somewhat rough so it looks like heavily whipped cream.

6. Bake meringues for 45 minutes, then turn oven off and leave meringues to cool in the oven. Peel circles off the paper and use as desired. I like simply to sandwich the meringue circles with 1 cup of whipped cream, sweetened to taste and colored with cocoa to the same

shade as the meringue. Drizzle the top with melted chocolate and pipe on rosettes of whipped cream.

VARIATION

Sandwich the meringue circles with Chocolate Parfait (page 23). Wrap the dessert in plastic and freeze to the point that you can cut it into wedges.

Chocolate Madeleines

Not as stodgy as ordinary made-leines, this chocolate version is crunchy on the exterior, moist and secretly fudgelike on the interior.

1. Preheat oven to 350 degrees. Lightly grease or butter the indentations of a madeleine mold.

2. Melt the butter and chocolate over low heat and stir until chocolate is melted. Set aside.

3. Combine cocoa, sugar, flour, and salt in a sauce pan.

4. In a bowl, lightly beat eggs, yolks, and vanilla together with a fork until well blended.

5. Stir chocolate mixture into the dry mixture, then add egg mixture and blend well. Place saucepan over very low heat and, stirring constantly, let the mixture warm for around 2 minutes. (It must not turn truly hot, so test with a finger to actu-

INGREDIENTS

1 stick plus 2 tablespoons unsalted butter
3 ounces semisweet chocolate
2 tablespoons cocoa powder
¾ cup granulated sugar
1¼ cups sifted all-purpose flour
Pinch salt
3 eggs plus 2 egg yolks
1 teaspoon vanilla extract

ally feel the temperature.) Remove from heat.

6. Fill the madeleine mold half full with batter. Do not over fill the indentations. Try for uniformity in size, especially if you are making Oysters and Pearls (see below). Bake 12 minutes. Turn out; cool.

VARIATION

To make Oysters and Pearls, a pretty pastry to accompany a bowl of dessert fruit or ice cream, simply place a large dollop of Cocoa Frosting (page 107) midway on the flat side of 1 madeleine cookie, then prop and wedge another cookie above it as if an oyster shell were half open. Let the frosting harden. Place a silver candy "pearl" at the tip of the shell. For a professional finish, brush the tops of the shells with melted chocolate.

Left to right: Chocolate Pretzels, page 127, Cocoa Potatoes, page 108, Oysters and Pearls, page 118, Chocolate Truffle Cakes, page 94

Whities

A chewy, thin white brownie. Try it for a change of pace.

YIELDS 12

INGREDIENTS

9 ounces white chocolate
1 stick unsalted butter
4 eggs
2 cups granulated sugar
1½ teaspoons vanilla extract
1 cup sifted all-purpose flour
½ teaspoon salt
⅔ cup slivered almonds

1. Preheat oven to 325 degrees. Butter and flour a 9 by 13-inch baking pan.

2. Grate or finely scrape 4 ounces of the chocolate and set aside. Melt remaining 5 ounces of chocolate over hot water (do not allow water to simmer). Melt the butter.

3. Beat the eggs, sugar, and vanilla together until thick and lemon colored. Stir in the melted chocolate and butter. Gently stir in flour and salt, and when batter is just blended, pour it into the prepared baking pan.

4. Scatter chocolate bits and slivered almonds on top of the batter, then bake for 30 to 35 minutes.

5. Let the whities cool in the pan, then cut them into squares.

Cookies

*L*ight and buttery, crisp and utterly delicious, these cookies in all shapes and forms glorify chocolate. Cocoa Balls and Chocolate Pretzels—with their shiny glaze and pearl-sugar "salt"—will surely become staples in your holiday repertoire. Bake the huge Chocolate Wafers dense with cocoa flavor and the crunch of brown sugar, then heap them in a rustic basket. Another crowd pleaser is a container of Chocolate Caramel Lollypop Cookies, sugary cookie bases baked on sticks, topped with caramel, then dipped in melted chocolate. And for everyday family goodness, bake Chocolate Chip Cookies with their healthy undiscernible bran.

Giant Crisp Chocolate Wafers

*H*uge, crisp, thin-as-a-tuile *wafers that are handsome served massed in a large basket. These could, of course, also be made in smaller dimensions.*

INGREDIENTS

¼ cup tightly packed light brown sugar
¼ cup granulated sugar
3 egg whites
2 tablespoons all-purpose flour
1 tablespoon cocoa powder
Pinch salt
Pinch powdered cinnamon
2 tablespoons heavy cream
4 tablespoons unsalted butter, melted
¼ teaspoon water
½ cup sliced almonds

1. Preheat oven to 325 degrees. Butter and flour a large, heavy, rimmed baking sheet, preferably cast-iron.

2. Whisk together the sugars and egg whites in a bowl. Add the flour, cocoa, salt, and cinnamon, and stir until well blended. Add cream and melted butter. Let mixture sit for 5 minutes.

3. Stir in the water. Spoon out 2 tablespoons of the mixture at one end of the baking sheet, and another 2 tablespoons at the other side. (On an 18 by 11-inch baking sheet, I only would attempt 2 cookies.) Spread the mixture out lightly from the center where it tends to be overthick.

The batter should be roughly 6 to 7 inches in diameter. The batter will expand, so leave room between cookies and around their edges. Scatter a few almonds on top of each.

4. Bake for 10 to 12 minutes. The cookies should just slightly darken at the edges. Remove baking sheet from oven and let cookies set briefly until firm enough to remove. Use a large spatula or pastry scraper to loosen the edges of the cookies, then lift them from the tray. Drape cookies over rolling pins or other objects so that each takes on a unique shape. Continue making cookies until batter is used up. Cool, then store at once in an airtight container if cookies are not to be eaten soon.

Cocoa Balls

Buttery soft inside and flaky crisp outside, these small cookies melt in your mouth.

1. Preheat the oven to 325 degrees.

2. Cream together the butter and sugar. Sift in the flour, salt, cocoa, and cinnamon. Add the vanilla and almonds and stir well. Shape dough into a ball.

3. To assure uniformity of size, divide the dough and cut it into quarters, then cut each quarter into 12 pieces. Take up each large marble-sized portion of dough and roll it briefly between your palms until a perfect ball has formed. Place the balls on an ungreased cookie sheet, leaving about ¾ inch between each cookie.

4. Bake for 12 to 14 minutes. The cookies should not brown on the bottom. Turn the tray if you have

YIELDS 48

INGREDIENTS

2 sticks unsalted butter
²/₃ cup confectioners' sugar, sifted after measuring
1¾ cups sifted all-purpose flour
½ teaspoon salt
6 tablespoons cocoa powder
Large pinch ground cinnamon
1 tablespoon vanilla extract
1 cup chopped blanched almonds, lightly toasted
2 ounces semisweet chocolate, melted (optional)

a known hot spot in your oven. The cookies will feel slightly soft still, but remove them from the tray to cool on a rack, where they will soon form a crisp exterior.

5. For a decorative touch, drizzle melted chocolate over.

Chocolate Chip Cookies

YIELDS 48

INGREDIENTS

2 sticks unsalted butter, at
  room temperature
¾ cup tightly packed light
  brown sugar
¾ cup granulated sugar
1 teaspoon vanilla extract
2 eggs
1 teaspoon salt
1 teaspoon baking soda
2¼ cups sifted all-purpose
  flour
12 ounces (2 cups)
  semisweet chocolate chips
½ cup finely chopped
  pecans
½ cup bran

*H*ere is the standard recipe for a
large batch of chocolate chip
cookies, the most popular cookie in
America. I changed only 1 ingredient, for with the addition of bran—
which is absolutely indistinguishable
herein—the cookies become good
sources of fiber which is sorely lacking in our diets.

1. Preheat the oven to 350
degrees.

2. Cream the butter, sugars,
and vanilla together until smooth,
then stir in the eggs. Add salt, baking
soda, and flour to the bowl and stir
until well blended. Stir in chocolate
chips, pecans, and bran.

3. Lightly grease 2 baking
sheets. Place portions of dough the
size of large walnuts on the pans and
press down lightly on the dough
with water-moistened fingers. Allow
for some expansion. Bake for 10 to
12 minutes.

VARIATION

For the chocolate lover, this is a
variation on the theme with extra
giant chocolate chips added. Unfor-
tunately, purchased milk chocolate
kisses will not work for these.

To make Kissy Cookies, have all
the ingredients for the master chocolate chip cookie recipe, but for the
chocolate, have 12 ounces of semisweet miniature chips and another 6
ounces of either miniature or regu-
lar semisweet chips: you should
have 18 ounces in all.

Stir 1¼ cups of miniature chips
into the cookie dough. Melt the remaining chips over hot water.

Place a sheet of parchment paper on a baking tray and anchor it
with a bit of chocolate between the
corners of the paper and the tray. Fit
a pastry bag with a small plain tube.
Fill the piping bag with chocolate

and press out ¾-inch drops of chocolate which are relatively flat, with
no tall point in the center. Let these
kisses harden in the refrigerator.

Place large portions of the
dough down on the greased baking
sheets and top with the large chips
before baking.

Chocolate Sugar Cookies

These round disks edged with pearl sugar are light, full of rich chocolate flavor, and crunchy.

1. Cream together the butter, sugar, salt, cinnamon, vanilla, and egg yolk. (This can be done by hand or machine.) When the mixture is light and creamy, stir in by hand the cocoa and flour. Mix until perfectly smooth.

2. On a flat surface lightly dusted with cocoa, roll the dough out beneath the palms of your hands to a cylinder that is an even 1½ inches in diameter. Place the dough roll on a platter, and cover snugly with plastic wrap. Refrigerate for at least 2 hours before cutting and baking them.

3. Preheat oven to 350 degrees. Remove the dough from the refrigerator and brush with a thick coating of egg yolk. Sprinkle the

YIELDS 36
INGREDIENTS

5 ounces unsalted butter, softened
½ cup granulated sugar
Pinch salt
Pinch ground cinnamon
1 teaspoon vanilla extract
1 egg yolk
⅓ cup cocoa powder, preferably Dutch process
1⅓ cups all-purpose flour, sifted after measuring
Cocoa powder for dusting

SUGAR COATING

1 egg yolk
⅓ cup pearl sugar (pär socker), available in speciality food stores

pearl sugar on a counter and roll the dough back and forth in the substance. The dough should be thickly coated with sugar.

4. Lightly grease a baking sheet. Cut the dough into ¼-inch-thick rounds. (I like to again roll the edge of each cookie in the sugar, so that the crystals can provide a white framework around the outer edge.) Place cookies on baking sheet (around 12 to a sheet, leaving room for expansion). Bake 10 minutes.

Chocolate Pretzels

These cookies are a nice addition to your holiday repertoire. Sporting a shiny chocolate glaze, they can further be "salted" with pearl sugar for a real pretzel look.

1. To make the cookie dough, cream together the butter and confectioners' sugar. Add the egg yolk, salt, and vanilla.

2. Sift together the flour and cocoa and add them to the butter. Stir and knead the mixture with your hands until it forms a smooth dough. Pack dough into a ball, cover tightly with plastic wrap, then refrigerate for at least 2 hours before using.

3. Preheat oven to 350 degrees. Lightly grease a baking sheet.

4. Remove dough from refrigerator and cut it into quarters. (It will need to soften slightly before it can be rolled.) Break off portions of dough and roll them with your hands on a surface lightly dusted with cocoa until they are long strands. The ropes of dough should be pencil thin and roughly 14 inches long. Twist the dough into pretzel shapes and place pretzels on baking sheet. (They don't spread much.) Bake cookies for 12 to 15 minutes, or until firm to the touch. Transfer cookies to cooling racks and prepare the rest of the cookies with the remaining dough.

5. To make the glaze, whisk together the egg white, cognac, lemon juice, water, confectioners' sugar, and cocoa. Brush warm pretzels with glaze and, if desired, sprinkle on the pearl sugar as "salt."

YIELDS 24
INGREDIENTS

2 sticks unsalted butter, softened
1 cup confectioners' sugar
1 egg yolk
¼ teaspoon salt
¼ teaspoon vanilla extract
1½ cups sifted all-purpose flour
⅓ cup cocoa powder, preferably Dutch process
Cocoa powder for dusting

GLAZE

1 egg white
1 tablespoon cognac or brandy
2 teaspoons lemon juice
2 tablespoons water
1⅓ cups confectioners' sugar, sifted after measuring
¼ cup cocoa powder, preferably Dutch process
Pearl sugar (pärl socker) (optional)

Brownie Cookies

Here is a valuable recipe. Rolled out and cut into shapes, the dough makes splendid cookies. Baked as a whole cookie sheet, then pulverized and mixed with butter, the cookie becomes a crumb crust useful for holding all types of cold fillings.

1. Melt the chocolate over hot water.

2. Sift the flour, baking soda, and baking powder together. Set aside.

3. In the bowl of a mixer, cream the butter. Add the sugar slowly and continue to beat. Add the vanilla, then the eggs 1 at a time. Add the chocolate and stir to blend.

4. Stir in the dry ingredients and the milk by hand. When just blended, mix in the walnuts. Cover and refrigerate dough for 30 minutes before rolling.

YIELDS 48

INGREDIENTS

4 ounces semisweet chocolate
1 ounce unsweetened chocolate
2¹/₃ cups sifted all-purpose flour
1¹/₂ teaspoons baking soda
¹/₂ teaspoon baking powder
1 stick unsalted butter
1 cup granulated sugar
1 tablespoon vanilla extract
2 eggs
1 tablespoon milk
³/₄ cup finely chopped walnuts

5. Preheat oven to 375 degrees. Lightly grease a cookie sheet.

6. To form the cookies, scoop out a portion of dough and roll out on a well-floured surface. When dough is ¼ inch thick, cut it into rounds or other desired shapes. Re-roll scraps and cut again.

7. Place on cookie sheet (leave room for expansion) and bake for 6 to 8 minutes. Watch for any hot spots in the oven and don't let these cookies overbrown.

VARIATION

For the Brownie Cookie Crust, make 1 recipe of Brownie Cookies and chill the dough briefly. Lightly grease the *back* side of a large baking sheet. Roll the dough out onto the baking sheet as thinly as possible so that the baked product will crumble easily. Bake crust at 375 degrees for 5 to 7 minutes.

Let crust harden, then slide the cookie from the sheet and cool completely. Roll over the cookie with a rolling pin until it is crushed to a fine crumb. (There should be about 2¼ cups of crumbs.)

Melt 1 stick plus 1 tablespoon of unsalted butter. Mix it into the crumbs and pack the mixture over the bottom and up the sides of a 10-inch springform pan. Freeze for 30 minutes before filling in order to set the crust. Try filling this crust with Kit's Chocolate Mousse (page 5); White Chocolate Mousse (page 4); ice cream, or other ideas.

Chocolate Chipped Brandy Snaps

A *chocolate variation on a classic theme, and a cookie that can be shaped and formed in useful ways.*

1. Preheat oven to 350 degrees. Liberally butter a baking sheet. Spoon 2 tablespoons of flour along the top rim of the pan, slant the pan down, and give it a good tap on a counter so that the flour slides smoothly and evenly over the entire surface of the pan.

2. Place butter, sugar, corn syrup, and ginger in a bowl and stir until blended. Add the flour and work into a smooth paste. (The easiest and most rapid method is simply to use your hand for the whole process rather than a spoon.) Last, add the chocolate chips and mix in.

3. Spoon 4 large walnut-sized pieces of paste onto the baking sheet, leaving 5 inches between each

YIELDS 20 TO 24

INGREDIENTS

1 stick unsalted butter,
  softened
1 cup granulated sugar
½ cup light corn syrup
1 generous teaspoon
  ground ginger
1 cup sifted all-purpose
  flour
1 cup miniature semisweet
  chocolate chips

portion. Moisten your hand with water and flatten each portion.

4. Bake for around 7 minutes. Set a timer on these cookies for 5 minutes, then keep a close watch. As the dough heats, they will spread into thin lacy circles of filigreed sugar, which caramalize rapidly. Let the cookies turn a deep gold, then remove at once from oven.

5. Keep testing 1 corner of the snaps with a spatula. If they are removed from the pan too soon, they will pull apart. When the perfect moment comes, they will lift off as firm but still warm wholes. Quickly remove them from the pan and let them drape over rolling pins or other forms which will allow them to set in interesting shapes. If the cookies harden too much, place the tray back in the oven to warm briefly.

6. Continue making remaining cookies until all the dough is used. Store absolutely airtight.

VARIATIONS

It is possible to make a multitude of shapes from this dough. For Ice Cream Dishes, place warm, round brandy snaps over the bottom of glass tumblers and press the sides down gently to form slight ruffles. Just before serving, place a scoop of ice cream in the cookie dish and top with Chocolate Toffee Sauce (page 171).

For Cannoli or Cream Horns, shape warm cookies around cream horn or cannoli tubes. When firm, pipe cookies full of whipped cream flavored with vanilla or coffee and sweetened to taste. Serve 2 to each person as dessert.

Chocolate Dollops

YIELDS 12

INGREDIENTS

6 tablespoons unsalted
   butter, at room
   temperature
½ cup tightly packed light
   brown sugar
½ cup granulated sugar
1 egg
1 cup milk
½ cup cocoa powder
1 teaspoon instant coffee
   powder
2 cups sifted all-purpose
   flour
1½ teaspoons baking soda
1 teaspoon salt
1 teaspoon vanilla extract

A nother 2-for-1 recipe. Make these cookies large and flat and you have cookie layers that can be sandwiched together with marshmallow frosting to make children's moon pies. Or make some domed caps fat and tall, and then some narrow stems, and you can create large chocolate mushrooms.

1.   Preheat the oven to 350 degrees.

2.   Cream together the butter and sugars. Add the egg and mix well, then stir in the milk.

3.   Add the cocoa and coffee flavorings, and when they are well blended, stir in the flour, soda, salt, and vanilla.

4.   These cookies are baked on an ungreased cookie sheet. At distances 6 inches from each other, place 6 heaping tablespoon scoops of dough. Dip your fingers in a cup of water and gently press and spread the batter out into 3-inch circles. Bake for 10 minutes, turning the tray as necessary if your oven has a hot spot.

5.   Run a spatula under each cookie and remove from tray to cool. Continue for remaining dough.

6.   To make the frosting, place the sugar and water in a small saucepan. Let the syrup boil until it reaches 230 degrees on a candy thermometer. While the syrup is boiling, from time to time wash down the sides of the pan with a pastry brush dipped in cold water.

7.   While the syrup boils, beat the egg white with an electric hand mixer until frothy, then sprinkle on the cream of tartar and continue beating until the egg white is very stiff. Add the marshmallows to the egg white.

8. Beating all the while, pour the syrup over the marshmallows and whites slowly, and continue beating until the frosting is stiff enough to spread.

9. Sandwich the cookies with marshmallow filling.

VARIATIONS

Chocolate Mushrooms: Make 1 batch of Chocolate Dollops and have ready ½ recipe of Cocoa Frosting (page 107). To form the mushrooms perfectly, place the batter in a pastry bag fitted with a ½-inch plain nozzle (though the cookies can also be formed by hand). To form the caps, pipe or shape 2-inch rounds that are slightly heaped in the center and tapered toward the edge. To form the stems, pipe out narrow strips of batter in a variety of mushroom stem-like lengths from 1 to 2½ inches. Have the end narrow, the other end

MARSHMALLOW FROSTING

1 cup granulated sugar
¼ cup water
1 egg white
¼ teaspoon cream of tartar
8 large marshmallows, cut in quarters, or 32 miniature marshmallows

doubled and fatter, curve some slightly to the left, others straight and to the right. Make an equal number of caps and stems.

Bake for 8 minutes, then remove the stems. Place aluminum foil over the caps and continue baking them another 3 to 4 minutes. Immediately as the caps are finished, press an indention in the underside with the blunt handle of a knife. Let the caps cool with their rounded sides up.

When cool, swirl Cocoa Frosting over the caps first, then attach the narrow stems into the cap indention with a dab of frosting. Prop mushrooms until the frosting hardens. The mushroom caps can be sprinkled lightly with sieved confectioners' sugar if so desired. Serve these mushrooms in a mushroom basket or on a tray covered with moss that has itself been sprinkled with confectioners'-sugar snow.

Chocolate Malted Cookies

Here is a good drop cookie with a distinctly malted taste. Both cookies and frosting use instant chocolate malted milk as a flavoring.

1. Melt the butter over low heat in a medium saucepan. Off the heat, stir the malted milk into the butter. Beat in the egg and stir until the mixture is smooth. Add salt and flour. Last, stir in the almonds. Cover the pan and place in the refrigerator to chill for 1 hour.

2. Preheat oven midway between 325 and 350 degrees. (If your oven is sluggish, heat to 350 degrees; if it tends to be overly hot, choose 325 degrees.) Butter a baking sheet.

3. Place level tablespoon-sized mounds of dough 2 inches apart on the baking sheet and flatten them slightly. The cookies will spread somewhat. Bake about 8 minutes. The cookies should not be allowed to blacken around the rim. Remove from baking sheet at once and cool.

4. Prepare the frosting. Place the butter and water in a small saucepan. Heat just until the butter has melted and the liquid comes to a simmer. Stir in the malted milk and the confectioners' sugar. Stir briskly until the frosting is smooth. The consistency can be regulated with a few drops of water if need be.

5. Frost the cookies while the mixture is still soft. Place the cookies on a rack to set the frosting.

YIELDS 20

INGREDIENTS

1 stick unsalted butter
1¼ cups instant chocolate malted milk
1 egg
¼ teaspoon salt
1 cup sifted all-purpose flour
½ cup ground blanched almonds

FROSTING

3 tablespoons unsalted butter
1 tablespoon water
⅓ cup instant chocolate malted milk
⅔ cup confectioners' sugar, sifted after measuring

Giant Crisp Chocolate Wafers, page 122

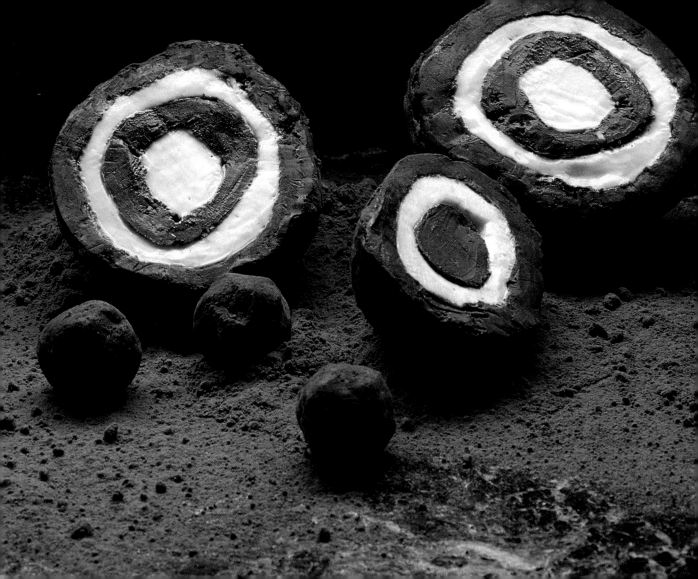

Toasted Coconut Chocolate Macaroons

These are crisp and airy chocolate creatures filled with the crunch of toasted coconut and almonds.

1. Preheat oven to 325 degrees. Oil or butter a cookie sheet.

2. Melt the chocolates over hot water. Set aside.

3. Separate the egg and combine the 2 egg whites. Beat whites with an electric mixer until they begin to stiffen. Slowly pour in the sugar and continue to beat the whites until they become stiff and glossy. Do not allow to overdry.

4. Stir the egg yolk and the vanilla into the melted chocolate. Add the coconut and almonds and mix well. Add the beaten egg whites and blend in gently until the dough is just mixed. It will be very stiff.

5. Drop by heaping tablespoons full onto the cookie sheet

YIELDS 24

INGREDIENTS

2 ounces unsweetened chocolate
4 ounces semisweet chocolate
1 egg plus 1 egg white
½ cup granulated sugar
1 teaspoon vanilla extract
1⅓ cups shredded coconut, lightly toasted
1⅓ cups shelled and blanched almonds, finely chopped and lightly toasted

leaving 2 inches between cookies. Bake for 18 minutes, then remove from the oven and let macaroons cool briefly on the pan. They will look and feel still moist.

6. Carefully remove macaroons and as soon as they are cool, they will harden. Store the cookies in an airtight container so they can retain their crisp exterior and moist, fudgelike interior.

Chocolate Caramel Lollypop Cookies

This confection-on-a-stick attempts to turn my favorite candy bar (Twix) into a cookie. Children adore these and adults too are amused when a basket of lollypop cookies is served along with raspberries, cream, and coffee for dessert.

1. Cream the butter, margarine, and sugar together. Stir in the egg, salt, vanilla, and malt.

2. Sift together the cornstarch, baking powder, and flour, and work into the butter mixture with the tips of your fingers, exactly as you would a pie crust. Do not overblend. Pack dough into a neat ball, cover with plastic wrap, and chill for at least 1 hour.

3. Preheat the oven to 350 degrees.

4. On a floured surface, roll the dough out to a thickness of ¼ inch. Cut out cookie rounds, using a

INGREDIENTS

4 tablespoons unsalted butter
4 tablespoons margarine or Crisco
1 cup granulated sugar
1 egg, lightly beaten
2 pinches salt
2 teaspoons vanilla extract
1 tablespoon instant malted milk
¼ cup cornstarch
1 teaspoon baking powder
1¾ cups sifted all-purpose flour
1 recipe Caramel (page 152)
10 ounces semisweet, couverture, or compound chocolate, approximately
Popsicle sticks (available at craft stores if not groceries)

3-inch round cutter. Lightly moisten the popsicle sticks with water and press 1 gently into each cookie. Moisten and press a scrap of dough over each stick and into the dough by its sides. Bake for 10 minutes, or until the cookies are a light gold. Remove from pan and cool.

5. Make the caramel filling. Let the caramel cool until it is very thick. (This process can be speeded by resting the pan in a bowl of ice water.)

6. Spread a thick layer of caramel over each cookie, taking care not to let it run over the edges. Place cookies on a tray and refrigerate until the caramel is firm.

7. Melt the chocolate over hot water. Use a pastry brush to brush the chocolate completely over the caramelized top sides of each cookie. When the top hardens you can, if you wish, coat the other side,

also. And it is possible to flick or twirl a pattern of chocolate on top of the lollypops. For further effect, wrap each cookie in foil or cellophane, and tie it under the cookie with a ribbon bow. Store the lollypops in a relatively cool spot so they remain firm and hard.

Chocolate Diamonds

YIELDS 24

INGREDIENTS

4 ounces unsweetened
  chocolate
1 pound confectioners'
  sugar
Large pinch powdered
  cinnamon
2 large or 3 medium egg
  whites
1 teaspoon vanilla extract
Granulated sugar

This is a peculiar recipe to make, but it results in a crisp half-meringue cookie that is delightful served with a tart fruit compote in summer or used as part of a Christmas cookie array. A nonstick baking pan is absolutely necessary here.

1. Melt the chocolate over warm water.

2. Stir half the sugar into the chocolate and mix well. The sugar will lump and ball, so use your fingertips to disperse the chocolate as well as possible. Stir the remaining sugar into the mixture and add the cinnamon.

3. Place a large sieve over a mixing bowl. Place the chocolate sugar into the sieve and press through, making sure all the small particles of chocolate are worked through the sieve.

4. Add the egg whites and vanilla to the sugar and stir until the mixture becomes a thick but still pliable dough. Refrigerate briefly.

5. Preheat oven to 260 degrees. Grease a nonstick baking sheet very lightly.

6. Sprinkle some granulated sugar on a counter. Take ¼ of the dough and roll it out ¼ inch thick. Use a cookie cutter or trace around a cardboard form to make diamonds. (Other simple heart or circle shapes could also be used.) Place cookies on baking sheet. Keep rolling and cutting cookies, regathering scraps and resugaring the surface as necessary until all are cut.

7. Bake for 45 minutes. At the end of the baking time, the slow oven should have caused the tops of the cookies to become just firm while the bottoms, puffed and expanded, turn to crisp meringue. Remove from the oven and let sit for 5 minutes before removing from tray. Cool and store in an airtight container.

Candies

*L*arge, easy candies that are quickly composed and handsomer than store bought fill this chapter. Here are piped Fruit and Nut Wreathes, Chocolate Glacéed Pears, giant Geodes composed of white and dark chocolates layered into spectacular rings, pecan Bear Paws full of rich caramel, and Preacher Balls (leave them refrigerated and they are chewy; let them dry in the air and they become sugary, melt-in-the-mouth morsels). At the end of the chapter are suggestions for the best box of homemade chocolates ever. Give the box to someone and you will have a friend for life!

Fruit and Nut Wreathes

Serve these easy, pretty sweets as after-dinner chocolates, or make a present of them at holiday time. Give a china manikin's hand with the chocolate rings gracing the fingers, or plant a small tree in a flower pot and hang the wreaths on the branches.

1. Melt the chocolate over hot water. Tear off a length of parchment paper to fit a baking sheet. Place dots of melted chocolate at the corners of the baking sheet and press paper onto the pan. Fit a pastry bag with a rosette tube.

2. Remove chocolate from the heat and stir continuously until it is glossy and lukewarm.

3. Put the chocolate into the pastry bag. Press out a small circle of chocolate about 3 to 3½ inches in diameter. Continue making wreathes until chocolate is used up.

YIELDS 16 TO 20

INGREDIENTS

*1 pound semisweet
   chocolate
Golden raisins
Muscat raisins
Hazelnuts
Slivered almonds
Candied pineapple, cut into
   small squares
Gold or silver dragées
   (fancies)*

4. Neatly arrange the raisins, nuts, candied fruit, and a few dragées on top of each wreath. Let the chocolates harden in a cool place, then remove them from the paper and store, covered, in a cool, dry place. Do not refrigerate or the chocolate might "bloom" with a film of gray discoloration.

Chocolate Glacéed Pears

These pears are delicious. Offer a basket of them for dessert sometime, with nothing else but coffee. Half of the fondant recipe (see page 144) coats quantities of pears, so I just give the basic procedure in this recipe. First prepare the fondant, then begin here.

1. Line some cookie sheets with wax paper.

2. The cookies are used to sandwich the pears and they should be no larger than the round bottoms of the pears. Fit each pear half with 1 cookie and trim the cookie to fit if necessary.

3. Melt the fondant over very low heat. Add brandy or vanilla to taste, but make sure that the flavoring is distinctly there.

4. Place a pear on a fork and dip it into the melted fondant. Place the chocolate side of a cookie

YIELDS 24

INGREDIENTS

2 packages Pepperidge
    Farm Orleans Cookies
24 large halves of glacéed
    pears
½ recipe Basic Fondant
Pear brandy or vanilla
    extract
1 pound Tobler
    Extra-Bittersweet
    Chocolate, or semisweet,
    couverture, or
    compound chocolate
Candied mint leaves
    (optional)

against the pear, then place the pear, cookie down, on the wax paper. Continue dipping pears. (It will probably be necessary to briefly reheat the fondant from time to time.) Let the pears sit at room temperature until the fondant hardens (around 2 hours on a dry day).

4. Chop the chocolate and melt it over hot water.

5. Use a pastry brush to brush one side of the pears with chocolate. Refrigerate the tray of pears briefly so that the chocolate can harden.

6. Take pears out of refrigerator, turn them over, and brush the other side with chocolate. Add a candied mint leaf to the top of each pear before the chocolate hardens. These pears keep nicely. Store covered in a cool but not cold place.

Double-Dipped Chocolate-Covered Cherries

That perennial favorite—chocolate-covered cherries—is especially succulent when double-dipped in chocolate as are these large, stemmed cherries. Note that cherries must dry overnight.

1. Drain the cherries. Pat cherries as dry as possible with paper toweling, then place them on a candy or cake rack covered with paper toweling and allow them to dry for at least 24 hours.

2. Cover a cookie sheet with wax paper.

3. I find it easiest to enrobe the cherries in fondant that has not been melted. Place a small pile of cornstarch on the counter and have handy a bowl of water and paper towels for wiping your hands. With cornstarch-dipped fingers, simply pull off a small portion of fondant,

YIELDS 3 TO 4 DOZEN CHERRIES

INGREDIENTS

2 bottles maraschino cherries with stems (such as Haddon House)
½ recipe fondant (page 144), flavored with Grand Marnier or kirsch
Cornstarch
12 ounces dark couverture or compound chocolate

flatten it a bit, and pat and wrap it around the cherry. (Be as careful as possible to leave the stem intact, but if it does fall off, simply stick it back down into the cherry and the chocolate will eventually hold it in place.) Place the fruit on the cookie sheet. Continue covering fruit in this manner. The cherries will need to be chocolate coated no later than 45 minutes after being covered in fondant, or the fondant will begin to melt. It is best not to do too many at once.

4. Melt the chocolate over hot water. For the most professional job, place cherries upside down, with their stems hanging down through the wires of a candy or cake rack. Press the fondant into a rounded shape if necessary, then coat the bottom halves of the cherries by brushing them with thick chocolate. Place the rack in the refrigerator for 5 minutes to harden the chocolate.

5. Place wax paper on a baking sheet.

6. Turn the cherries right side up on the rack. Place a fork under a cherry and dip the fruit in the chocolate. Place cherries on the paper-lined baking sheet. When all the cherries have been dipped, refrigerate the tray briefly.

7. To double-dip the cherries, spoon chocolate over the upright cherries and swirl the chocolate around the stem in a pretty whisp of a pattern. Then take a pastry brush and coat the stems with chocolate.

8. Place cherries in fluted candy cases when hard. Place in a covered container and keep in a cool place for 2 weeks to mellow. At the end of this time, the fondant will have melted and transformed itself into a liquor.

Basic Fondant

The preceding 2 recipes require fondant. Correctly stored, fondant keeps a long time, so make a large amount. Use half to coat the glacéed pears, the other half to enrobe the stemmed cherries.

INGREDIENTS

4 cups granulated sugar
1½ cups cold water
¼ teaspoon cream of tartar
Kirsch or Grand Marnier

1. Clear a large space on a counter or marble pastry slab. Splash it with cold water, and have a cup of cold water and a clean pastry brush near the stove.

2. Place the sugar and water into a saucepan. Stir over very low heat until the sugar has melted and the liquid is clear. Turn up the heat and continue stirring until the syrup reaches a boil. Stop stirring and add the cream of tartar. Dip the pastry brush in cold water and wash down the sides of the pan, then immediately cover the pan and let the syrup boil vigorously for 3 minutes. Uncover, insert a thermometer, and let cook rapidly to the soft-ball stage (240 degrees).

3. Immediately take the saucepan to the counter or slab. Run a wet hand over the moist surface to redampen any dry spots, then carefully pour out the syrup onto the counter. Do not pour out the last bit of syrup and do not scrape the pan clean. (That would add overcooked, crystallized sugar.)

4. Let the syrup cool. To work the syrup most effectively, have 2 scrapers at hand: either wooden or metal spatulas do nicely. Start scraping the outer portions of syrup into the center and keep turning the mass over and over itself until it starts stiffening and lightening in color. Keep working the sugar until it is perfectly white and so thick that it can be kneaded. Knead briefly, then divide into 2 portions.

5. Flavor half with kirsch or Grand Marnier to taste. (Simply sprinkle on the flavoring and knead it in.) Leave the other portion unflavored. Wrap both fondants tightly in plastic wrap and place them in a covered container. Moisten 2 sheets of paper toweling and fit them over the fondant. Cover the dish with the lid and let the fondant mellow in the refrigerator for at least 4 days before using.

White Chocolate "Ravioli" with Hazelnut Filling

YIELDS 25

INGREDIENTS

½ cup shelled whole hazelnuts
2 ounces semisweet chocolate
2 tablespoons unsalted butter
1 tablespoon granulated sugar
1 tablespoon brandy or rum
9 ounces Tobler Narcisse white chocolate, grated

*H*ere is an easy and delicious fool-the-eye candy a batch of which, along with a crinkle-edged ravioli cutter, would make a small clever present.

1. Preheat oven to 350 degrees. Form a sheet of tinfoil over the back of a 9-inch square baking pan. Place the foil in the pan and smooth it into corners and sides as evenly as possible.

2. Place the hazelnuts in a roasting pan. Put them in oven and roast for 10 minutes, then place nuts in a heavy kitchen towel and rub them back and forth vigorously, so that their bitter dried skins are removed. Pick over and discard all skins. Grind the nuts coarsely or chop in a food processor.

3. Melt the dark chocolate and butter over hot water. Stir in sugar, brandy, and nuts, and mix well. Form paste into 25 small balls.

4. Arrange the chocolate balls in 5 even rows over the bottom of the dish, and press each ball down so that it is somewhat flattened against the bottom of the pan.

5. Place the grated white chocolate over hot water and let it melt completely. Stir until smooth, then immediately pour the chocolate into the center of the pan and over as many chocolate rounds as possible. Using a finger, smooth the chocolate evenly over the balls, out to the edge of the pan in a thin, flat layer.

6. Place the pan in refrigerator briefly, until the chocolate hardens somewhat but does not completely firm. Run a knife or ravioli cutter between the rows and down the sides, then replace dish in the refrigerator to harden. When firm, lift out the foil and separate the candies into individual pieces.

Chocolate Truffles

Here is a rich chocolate truffle recipe. It is also one of the components of the following recipe for giant Geodes.

1.   Put cream and butter into a saucepan. Let butter melt over medium heat then, stirring all the while, turn up the heat and let the cream just come to a boil.

2.   Off the heat, add the chocolate to the saucepan and stir until it is completely melted. Continue stirring until the mixture thickens and cools somewhat. Stir in the Grand Marnier, then cover mixture and place in the refrigerator. Let the mixture thicken for at least 2 hours but stir it 3 or 4 times as it cools and hardens.

3.   To form the truffles, scoop up portions of the chocolate with a spoon. Dust a surface thickly with cocoa, then also with cocoa-dusted

YIELDS AROUND 50

INGREDIENTS

1²/₃ cups heavy cream
7 tablespoons unsalted butter
1 pound semisweet chocolate, cut or broken into pieces
2 tablespoons Grand Marnier (or to taste)
Cocoa powder for dusting

palms, roll the chocolate portions between your hands to make balls. Roll the balls in cocoa, refrigerate them again immediately.

Geodes

Although these creations have no cavity in the middle lined with crystals, the name geode *still seems appropriate, for when this giant layered truffle is cut in half, it looks like some of those handsome rocks. You can make a huge geode 5 to 6 inches in diameter, or several smaller 2- to 3-inch ones. You can even place a chocolate cordial in the middle if you wish. These make splendid gifts.*

1. Have the chocolate truffle mixture cooling in the refrigerator.

2. Place the white chocolate in a pan over hot water. Add the boiling water to the chocolate and whisk over heat until the mixture is perfectly smooth.

3. Continue beating the white chocolate until it thickens somewhat, then leave it to cool at room temperature. You should have both

YIELDS 2 LARGE OR SEVERAL SMALLER

INGREDIENTS

1 recipe Chocolate Truffles (page 147)
12 ounces white chocolate, grated
¹⁄₃ cup plus 2 tablespoons boiling water, approximately
Confectioners' sugar as needed
Semisweet, bittersweet, or couverture chocolate, melted and cooled slightly
Cocoa powder

chocolate mixtures at the same packing and firming consistency. (Do *not* refrigerate the white chocolate as it will harden too much.) If necessary, add a little confectioners' sugar to solidify the white chocolate.

4. To make 2 large geodes, form 1 white and 1 brown ball, each 1 inch in diameter. Wrap the white ball in some brown truffle mixture and place in the freezer; wrap the brown ball in white chocolate. Continue building each truffle with layers of alternating colors, smoothing each layer as much as possible and occasionally placing the balls in the freezer to solidify. When the mixtures are used up, place the geodes in the freezer to harden.

5. To make smaller geodes, form several balls of alternating colors and build them up, but with fewer layers. Chill.

6. Brush geodes with melted chocolate and roll in cocoa. Wrap and refrigerate at least 1 day.

7. To serve, slice the large geodes in half and place them on a platter; each guest cuts a wedged portion for himself. Place smaller geodes on a platter for individual and halved portions.

Chocolate Malteds

*F*ast, easy, slightly chewy little candies.

1. Melt the butter and cream together, and when the liquid cools slightly, stir in the vanilla. Add the malted milk and sugar and stir well.

2. With your fingers, knead the mixture briefly, then press and form the chocolate into 1-inch-round balls. Let dry for 30 minutes, then roll in cocoa. Leave out to dry overnight.

3. Melt the chocolate over hot water, then dip in the candies to coat them. Drizzle a "string" of chocolate off the end of a spoon to make a small pattern on the chocolate. Let harden in refrigerator.

YIELDS 18

INGREDIENTS

4 tablespoons unsalted
   butter
2 tablespoons heavy cream
¼ teaspoon vanilla extract
1 cup instant chocolate
   malted milk
⅓ cup granulated sugar
Cocoa powder for dusting
8 ounces semisweet,
   couverture, or dark
   compound chocolate

An Elegant Cluster of Grapes, page 155

Pecan Butter Fudge

A grainy, old-fashioned fudge.

1. Butter a 9- or 10-inch square baking pan.

2. Place the butter and cream in a saucepan over very low heat and stir until the butter has melted.

3. Add the sugar, cocoa, and salt, and stir continuously until the mixture comes to a slow, rolling boil, then time the fudge for 8 minutes. Stir occasionally and briefly while the fudge cooks. Have a cup of cold water ready, and at the end of 8 minutes, drop a bit of fudge into the water. It should form a medium-firm ball. If the ball seems a bit soft, continue cooking for another 2 minutes, but the entire cooking time after boil is reached should not exceed 9 minutes.

On dish (clockwise from top): Preacher Balls, page 154, Fruit and Nut Wreaths, page 140, Chocolate Glacéed Pears, page 141, Double-Dipped Chocolate-Covered Cherries, page 142

YIELDS 1½ POUNDS

INGREDIENTS

3 tablespoons unsalted butter
½ cup heavy cream
2½ cups granulated sugar
6 tablespoons cocoa powder
Pinch salt
1 teaspoon vanilla extract
⅔ cup shelled pecans, broken roughly in half

4. Remove fudge from the heat and stir in the vanilla and pecans. Continue beating the fudge until it has thickened to the consistency of a sluggish molasses, then quickly scrape the fudge into the buttered pan while it is still pourable. The fudge should have a nice gloss to it. Chill until firm. Cut into squares and serve.

Bear Paws

*T*hese are large, paw-shaped versions of the classic pecan and caramel Turtles. For an amusing presentation, place the candies in a walking paw print pattern across a large white serving tray.

1. To make the caramel, combine the sugar, corn syrup, and half the cream in a heavy saucepan. Cook over gentle heat for 10 minutes. Add the remaining cream slowly and continue cooking for another 5 minutes at a low rolling boil.

2. Add the butter, bit by bit, then insert a candy thermometer. Reduce the heat somewhat and let the caramel slowly cook until it reaches 244 degrees on a candy thermometer. Remove the pan from the heat and gently stir in the vanilla and salt. Set aside for 10 minutes.

3. Cover 2 cookie sheets with wax or parchment paper. For each

YIELDS 24

INGREDIENTS

144 large shelled pecans (approximately 1/2 pound)
12 ounces semisweet, couverture, or dark compound chocolate, grated

CARAMEL

1 cup granulated sugar
1/2 cup corn syrup
1 cup heavy cream
2 1/2 tablespoons unsalted butter, chilled and cut in pieces
1/2 teaspoon vanilla extract
1/4 teaspoon salt

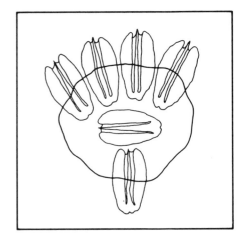

bear paw, arrange 4 nut "toes" in a semicircle, place a nut turned sideways in the curve of the circle, then place a nut lengthwise under it as a "heel." Each bear paw will require 6 nuts to make 24 3-inch paws.

4. When the caramel has cooled for 10 minutes, spoon out globs of it in the middle of each cluster. Place the trays to harden in a

refrigerator. (The caramel can be pressed into shape somewhat as it chills.) When the caramels are cool, peel them from the paper. Turn paper over and replace it on the baking sheets.

5. Melt chocolate over hot water. When it has melted, stir it briskly. Place a caramel with the bottom side up on a fork (preferably a 2-pronged fork). Dip the top of the caramel generously in the chocolate and place the candy chocolate side up on the baking sheet. Repeat for remaining candies. Let the chocolates harden, then box and store them in a cool, dry place.

Preacher Balls

This is a very old recipe that, I suppose, received its name less from the spirituality of the ingredients than from the fact that these sticky candies were once, with their grained base, inexpensive enough for frugal parsons. Today their claim to virtue (other than ease and goodness), is that little energy is used to produce them.

1. Lightly grease a baking sheet or a large pan with sides.

2. Combine the butter, sugar, and milk in a saucepan. Let come to a boil over medium heat, then continue cooking at a slow boil for 3 minutes. Remove pan from the heat and immediately stir in cocoa, then oatmeal, ground nuts, and vanilla. Mix everything well.

3. Pour the batter into the prepared pan. Cool briefly, then refrig-

YIELDS 36

INGREDIENTS

1 stick unsalted butter
2 cups granulated sugar
1/2 cup milk
1/2 cup cocoa powder
2 cups oatmeal (not instant)
1/2 cup ground almonds or pecans
1 teaspoon vanilla extract
1 1/4 cups sliced almonds

erate until the candy hardens somewhat and you can handle it.

4. While the candy cools, toast the sliced almonds in a frying pan or under a broiler until they are light brown. Chop them lightly with a food processor or a knife until they are coarse dice.

5. Scoop up a portion of candy the size of a large marble and roll it between the palms of your hands until it is perfectly smooth. Roll in the chopped almonds and then refrigerate the balls until hard.

6. Store Preacher Balls in an airtight container in the refrigerator. If these are kept refrigerated, they remain very chewy. If they are left out to dry, they become crisp and sugary. Both versions are delicious.

VARIATION

An Elegant Cluster of Grapes:
Make the Preacher Balls and roll
them until perfectly smooth. Make
some slightly smaller than others so
that there are a variety of sizes. Roll
the balls in cocoa instead of nuts,
and chill them completely.

Arrange the balls in a cluster on
a small serving platter, with the
smallest balls at the bottom, the larger balls stacked toward the top.

Melt 4 ounces of semisweet or
compound chocolate over hot
water. Line a cookie sheet with aluminum foil. Select a very large ivy or
grape leaf, and brush the melted
chocolate over the back of the leaf.
Place leaf on cookie sheet.

Scoop the remaining chocolate
into a small paper piping bag (see
page xviii), and make a rough grape
stem 3 inches long and ¾ inch wide,
with a slight curve to it. Pipe out a
long spiraling tendril. Place the

cookie sheet in the refrigerator to
harden for 5 minutes.

Peel off the leaf from the chocolate and remove the stem and tendril. Arrange them at the top of the
cluster. This is a handsome presentation to serve with coffee after a formal dinner.

NOTE

The cluster of grapes may also be
made with Chocolate Truffles (page
147).

155

Chocolate Macadamia Nut Toffee

Here is a good toffee with an exotic substitution of macadamia nuts for the usual almonds.

1. Butter a 9 by 13-inch baking pan and set aside.

2. Brush off any salt from the roasted macadamias. Cut each nut roughly in half.

3. Melt the butter in a saucepan. Add the sugar, water, and corn syrup, and place a candy thermometer in the pan. Cook over medium heat at a low, rolling boil, stirring occasionally. When the mixture reaches 300 degrees on the thermometer, quickly add the macadamia halves, swirl the pan vigorously, and pour out the mixture into the buttered pan. Spread the candy as evenly as possible. Let it harden until completely firm.

YIELDS 2 POUNDS

INGREDIENTS

1 cup roasted macadamia nuts (not raw nuts)
2 sticks unsalted butter
1½ cups granulated sugar
3 tablespoons water
1 tablespoon corn syrup
9 ounces bittersweet chocolate, cut into pieces
¾ cup finely chopped macadamia nuts

4. Turn the candy out and wipe any excess butter from the smooth bottom side.

5. Melt the chocolate over hot water. Pour and brush the chocolate thickly over the bottom of the candy and press in the chopped macadamias. Let harden.

6. You can, if you wish, use more chocolate and coat the top side also, but I like the looks of the single coating for this recipe. Break the candy into large portions and store, covered, in the refrigerator.

A Box of Sweetmeats

This is a collection of chocolates that I would love to give or get for a special present. Because they are twice as large as most candies, they make a spectacular gift, each delectable placed in a large gold-foil case and all cases displayed in a candy box.

1.   2 Chocolate Glacéed Pears (page 141), coated in extra bittersweet chocolate.

2.   2 cases holding 2 Double-Dipped Chocolate-Covered Cherries (page 142), with the 2 cherry stems in each case linked together with drops of chocolate at the top.

3.   2 cases holding clusters of cocoa-coated Preacher Balls (page 154). Make the balls very small and let them dry for a day out of the refrigerator. Place a small chocolate leaf at the side of each cluster.

4.   2 miniature Fruit and Nut Wreathes (page 140).

5.   A 2-inch Geode (page 148), white on the outside, sliced in half and placed in a case.

6.   2 rough chunks of Chocolate Macadamia Nut Toffee (page 156), with chopped macadamias on the outside.

7.   2 large pieces Pecan Butter Fudge (page 153).

8.   2 or 3 large Chocolate Malteds (page 150), each ball wrapped tightly in gold foil.

9.   2 Bear Paws (page 152).

10.   1 large, plain dark Chocolate Truffle (page 147), rolled in finely chopped green pistachio nuts.

Oh yes.

More Chocolate Delights

*T*his chapter should win an award for The Most: the most chocolate possible in an Egg Cream Soda or malted, the thickest, richest flavor possible in a chocolate drink (Hot Mexican Chocolate), the densest chocolate texture in an ice cream without it turning to candy (Fudge Ice Cream), the most sensuous ice cream (Orange Flower Ice Cream with Bittersweet Chocolate Bits), the most festive frozen dessert into which to stick candles and celebrate (Frozen Cassata Torte). Prepare any of these and give yourself a blue ribbon topped with a Chocolate Autograph.

Hot Mexican Chocolate

A thick exotic brew that is most sustaining on a cold winter's day. In Mexico, it would be whipped to a froth with a molinillo, *a grooved wooden-whisk that is rubbed rapidly back and forth between the palms.*

1. Place the grated chocolate in a medium saucepan and melt over hot water. Add the boiling water and mix well. Stir in the warm milk and cream (they can be heated gently together), then add the sugar, spices, and salt.

2. Whisk mixture over medium-low heat until the mixture comes to a boil, then regulate to a simmer and cook for 5 minutes, whisking all the time. Remove from heat and sieve through a fine strainer. (The chocolate can be prepared ahead to this point.)

3. In a bowl, beat the egg and vanilla together until frothy. Reheat

SERVES 4

INGREDIENTS

2 ounces unsweetened chocolate, grated
¼ cup boiling water
2 cups milk, warmed
1 cup heavy cream, warmed
3 tablespoons granulated sugar
1 teaspoon powdered cinnamon
Pinch powdered cloves
Pinch salt
1 egg
1¼ teaspoons vanilla extract

the chocolate mixture if it has cooled. Slowly add a ladle of hot chocolate to the egg, beating all the while, then add egg to the remaining chocolate. Beat with an electric hand mixer or an old-fashioned rotary whisk (even better), for 3 minutes over low heat.

When nicely frothy, pour the drink into 4 coffee cups and serve immediately.

Deluxe
Chocolate Egg Cream Soda

The richest, most delicious soda in the world.

1. Have 2 soda glasses frosted in the freezer.

2. Melt the chocolate over hot water. Stir in the chocolate syrup and mix well. Let cool to room temperature.

3. Place the chocolate syrup, egg, half 'n half, and 1 large scoop of chocolate ice cream in a blender and blend 1 minute. Divide the mixture between the 2 glasses.

4. Add approximately ⅔ cup soda water to each glass and stir briskly with a spoon. Drop 2 large scoops of vanilla ice cream into each glass, then top off the glasses with soda water until the froth just starts to spill over.

5. Stick a straw in each glass and place glasses on dessert plates.

SERVES 2

INGREDIENTS

2 ounces bittersweet
  chocolate
½ cup chocolate syrup
1 egg
⅔ cup half 'n half
Dark chocolate ice cream,
  such as Baskin-Robbins'
  Chocolate Fudge
Ice cold soda water
Rich vanilla ice cream,
  such as Baskin-Robbins'
  French Vanilla
Soda crackers

Serve with soda crackers on each plate.

Dark Chocolate Malted

*T*he most flavorful, darkest chocolate malted imaginable.

1. Place 2 soda glasses or brandy snifters in the freezer to frost.

2. Melt the solid chocolate
over hot water. Add the chocolate
syrup and stir briefly over heat until
the chocolates are well mixed. Let
cool to room temperature in the refrigerator.

3. Place the chocolate syrup,
ice cream, milk, and malt in a blender, and whirl to a thick, smooth
cream. Pour into chilled glasses.

SERVES 2

INGREDIENTS

*1 ounce bittersweet or
semisweet chocolate, cut
into bits*
*¼ cup chocolate syrup,
preferably Hershey's*
*12 ounces dark chocolate
ice cream, such as
Baskin-Robbins'
Chocolate Fudge*
½ cup chocolate milk
*1 tablespoon
chocolate-flavored malt*

Fudge Ice Cream

A rich, sticky-thick ice cream.

1. Combine yolks, half 'n half, sugar, and salt in a heavy saucepan. Place over medium heat and stir constantly until the mixture thickens and coats a spoon. (Do not allow custard to approach a boil.)

2. Off the heat, add the butter and stir constantly until the butter is all melted and perfectly amalgamated into the custard. Place in refrigerator and stir from time to time until the custard reaches room temperature.

3. Melt the chocolates over hot water, then allow to cool.

4. When the custard is the correct temperature, stir in the chocolate. Add the cinnamon, vanilla, and cream and stir until smooth.

YIELDS 1½ QUARTS

INGREDIENTS

8 egg yolks
1½ cups half 'n half
⅔ cup granulated sugar
¼ teaspoon salt
6 tablespoons unsalted butter, chilled and cut in pieces
5 ounces semisweet chocolate
3 ounces unsweetened chocolate
Pinch ground cinnamon
1 tablespoon vanilla extract
2 cups heavy cream, well chilled

5. Place custard mixture in ice cream freezer and follow manufacturer's instructions for churning the ice cream. When ice cream is finished, pack into containers and freeze.

Mocha Ice Cream

Taste this ice cream base carefully for flavoring. What you want is a perfect balance of chocolate and coffee, those happy companions.

1. Melt the chocolate over hot water.

2. Combine yolks, half 'n half, sugar, and salt in a heavy saucepan. Place over medium heat and stir constantly until the mixture thickens and coats a spoon. (Do not allow to come to or near a boil.)

3. Off the heat, add the butter, melted chocolate, and coffee, and stir until the butter melts into the custard. Place in the refrigerator and let cool until the custard reaches room temperature. Stir occasionally to prevent a skin forming.

4. Stir in the cream. Taste and add more coffee if the chocolate predominates. Place custard in an ice cream maker and churn accord-

YIELDS 1½ QUARTS

INGREDIENTS

6 ounces bittersweet
   chocolate
8 egg yolks
1½ cups half 'n half
⅔ cup granulated sugar
Large pinch salt
6 tablespoons unsalted
   butter, chilled and cut in
   pieces
1½ tablespoons instant
   espresso coffee powder
2 cups heavy cream, well
   chilled
Grated chocolate or
   chocolate-coated mocha
   beans

ing to manufacturer's directions. When finished, pack into containers and freeze.

5. Serve portions of ice cream topped with grated chocolate or a chocolate-coated mocha bean.

Orange Flower Ice Cream with Bittersweet Chocolate Bits

A heady, aromatic ice cream that is dazzling on the palate. It can be prettily served in a large, hollowed-out orange, with a cluster of orange blossoms or white freesia on the side to complement and enhance the sensuous pleasure.

1. Mix yolks, half 'n half, sugar, and salt in a heavy saucepan. Stir continuously over medium heat until the custard coats the back of a spoon.

2. Add the butter off the heat, and stir the custard constantly until the butter melts. Let the custard cool in the refrigerator to room temperature and stir it from time to time as it cools.

3. Add the heavy cream, orange flower water, Grand Marnier, and chocolate bits. Stir, then place in ice cream maker and churn according to manufacturer's directions.

YIELDS 1 QUART

INGREDIENTS

6 egg yolks
1 cup half 'n half
½ cup granulated sugar
¼ teaspoon salt
4 tablespoons unsalted
    butter
1½ cups heavy cream, well
    chilled
2½ tablespoons orange
    flower water
2 tablespoons orange
    liqueur, preferably Grand
    Marnier
2 ounces bittersweet
    chocolate, cut in tiny bits

When finished, pack in containers and freeze.

Frozen Cassata Torte

A festive Italian ice cream dessert with a chocolate candy crust. Make it up to a week ahead and keep it stored in the freezer.

1. Butter or oil a 9- or 10-inch springform pan. Cut a circle of wax paper and fit it into the bottom of the pan. Place pan in freezer.

2. To make the crust, combine chocolate chips, butter, and cream in the top of a double boiler. Heat until the chocolate has melted, then remove from heat and add cinnamon and almonds. Stir until well blended and smooth, then place pan in refrigerator and, stirring from time to time, let the mixture cool and thicken to a peanut butterlike paste.

3. Rapidly spread and smooth the chocolate paste into the cold prepared pan, over the bottom and up the sides to a height of 1¼

SERVES 12

INGREDIENTS

4 ounces semisweet
   chocolate
1 pound ricotta
2 cups heavy cream
½ cup granulated sugar
½ cup finely chopped
   almonds
¼ cup amaretto
2 teaspoons vanilla extract
2 tablespoons cocoa
   powder
½ cup semisweet miniature
   chocolate chips
¼ teaspoon ground
   cinnamon
1 teaspoon finely grated
   lemon zest
¾ cup mixed candied and
   dried fruits (red and
   green cherry halves,
   candied orange or
   pineapple, golden
   raisins)
Chocolate shavings or curls
Whipped cream

inches. Place pan back in the freezer.

4. To make the filling, melt the chocolate over hot water.

5. Place the ricotta, cream, and sugar in the bowl of an electric mixer. Whip until thick but not totally stiff. Remove from mixer and stir in almonds, amaretto, and vanilla. Spoon half the mixture into another bowl.

6. To half of the ricotta cream, add the melted chocolate, cocoa, chocolate chips, and cinnamon. Mix well, then spoon into the chocolate pie shell and mound it up in the center so that the chocolate is thickest in the middle and tapers down to the inner edge of the shell. Replace in freezer.

7. To the other half of the ricotta, add the lemon zest and ½ cup fruit; mix well. Remove the torte

from the freezer and spread the white cream evenly over the chocolate so that the top of the torte is flat. Scatter the remaining fruit over the surface. Cover with foil and replace in freezer until needed. (If you intend to keep this dessert for up to a week before use, place the springform pan in a plastic bag and tie securely.)

8.   To unmold, let the torte sit at room temperature for 15 minutes. Run a knife firmly around the edge and release the side. Lift the bottom of the mold off the torte, then peel off the wax paper. Place the torte on a serving platter.

9.   Trim the rim of the chocolate crust even with a knife if it is misshapen. To garnish, heap a mound of grated chocolate on the top. You could also pipe rosettes of whipped cream around the edge.

CRUST

1¹/₂ cups semisweet chocolate chips
4 tablespoons unsalted butter
¹/₃ cup heavy cream
¹/₄ teaspoon ground cinnamon
1¹/₂ cups finely chopped almonds (with skins)

10.   After the torte has remained at room temperature for around 40 minutes, the top white layer will be soft and creamy, the chocolate layer still frozen, and the crust, chewy: an interesting variety of textures. Refrigerate at this point if you like, or let the torte sit another hour or so, at which time both white and chocolate layers will be soft.

Snowball Pie

*R*ich vanilla ice cream, toasted coconut, and fudge ice cream packed into a delicious coconut crust—topped, of course, with hot fudge sauce. I am not sure but that this is somewhat morally compromising.

1. To make the crust, cream together the butter and sugar. Add and blend in the egg yolk, then work in the flour. Knead in the coconut by hand.

2. Pack the dough into a ball and refrigerate for 30 minutes.

3. Preheat oven to 350 degrees. Roll out the dough onto a floured surface and line a 10-inch tart or pie tin. (You may have to do some pinching and pressing to the soft dough.) Gently fit a sheet of greased foil over the dough and fill the shell with beans or other weights. Bake the crust blind for 12

SERVES 12

INGREDIENTS

1 quart rich chocolate ice cream (like Baskin-Robbins' dark fudge variety), softened
1 quart rich vanilla ice cream
6 ounces shredded coconut, lightly toasted
Double recipe of Hot Fudge Sauce (page 172)

COCONUT CRUST

1/3 cup unsalted butter
3 tablespoons granulated sugar
1 egg yolk
3/4 cup all-purpose flour, sifted after measuring
1 cup flaked coconut

minutes. Lift out the foil and weights and continue baking the shell for another 15 minutes or until the shell is golden. (Protect rim with foil if it threatens to overbrown.) Cool pie shell briefly, then lift out of the baking dish to cool completely on a cake rack.

4. To assemble, spread the softened chocolate ice cream into the shell. Use an ice cream scoop to make half rounds of vanilla ice cream and place them over the top of the chocolate layer. (The pie can be frozen at this point.)

5. Let pie soften slightly before serving. Immediately before serving, sprinkle on the toasted coconut. Serve the Hot Fudge Sauce on the side.

Mississippi Mud Pie

*H*ere is an easy, frozen, southern concoction. Pull it out of the freezer on a hot evening and let guests delight in its sophisticated mixture of chocolate, coffee, and liqueurs. This will freeze well for 2 weeks.

1. Break the cookies into small portions. Place cookies in a food processor and blend until the crumbs are finely textured. Mix in the melted butter. Press the crumbs into a 10-inch pie plate. Place crust in freezer while preparing the filling.

2. Place the softened ice creams in a large bowl. Stir in the coffee, liqueur, and brandy and mix until completely blended. Pour the thick mixture into the crust, then return the pie to the freezer and allow to freeze solidly. If pie is not to be eaten within the day, cover with freezer wrap to preserve freshness.

SERVES 8 TO 10

INGREDIENTS

1 quart dark fudge ice cream (purchased or *Fudge Ice Cream, page 163*), softened
1 quart coffee ice cream (purchased or *Mocha Ice Cream, page 164*), softened
2 tablespoons instant coffee powder
2 tablespoons coffee liqueur
3 tablespoons brandy or cognac
Whipped cream (optional)
Chocolate shavings (optional)
2 recipes Chocolate Toffee Sauce (page 171)

CRUST

22 Oreo cookies
2 tablespoons unsalted butter, melted

3. Remove the pie from the freezer approximately 15 minutes before serving. Decorate with rosettes of whipped cream and chocolate shavings if desired. Place a pitcher of Chocolate Toffee Sauce on the side and let each diner pour on his own sauce.

Nouvelle Chocolate Sauce

A fashionable and useful thin chocolate sauce, the kind that floats to the rim of a plate in many nouvelle cuisine *desserts.*

1. Melt the chocolate with the water over low heat. Add the sugar and stir until it dissolves. Bring the sauce to a simmer and stir continuously for 2 minutes.

2. Remove pan from the heat and let chocolate cool briefly, then add the cognac. Strain sauce through a fine sieve and cool to room temperature.

NOTE

This sauce will need to be regulated with more water to make it the correct pouring and floating consistency. It should be similar to light (unwhipped) cream. This sauce should be served at room temperature or just slightly cool, and it can be made ahead, refrigerated, then thinned with water before use.

YIELDS 2½ CUPS

INGREDIENTS

9 ounces bittersweet chocolate
1½ cups water
½ cup granulated sugar
1½ teaspoons cognac or brandy

Chocolate Toffee Sauce

A good, not overly sweet sauce that contains small crunchy portions of toffee candy.

1. Place the chocolate and water in a small saucepan and melt the chocolate over very low heat, stirring constantly. Stir in the sugar and continue to cook and stir for another 2 minutes, or until the mixture has somewhat thickened.

2. Off the heat, add the butter and let it dissolve into the sauce. Stir in the vanilla and then the toffee bits. Serve hot or warm.

NOTE

This sauce can be kept in the refrigerator for a week. Warm it gently to bring it to pouring consistency before use, but once the toffee is in, the sauce must not actually overheat or the toffee will melt.

YIELDS 2 CUPS

INGREDIENTS

4 squares unsweetened chocolate, chopped
⅔ cup cold water
⅓ cup granulated sugar
3 tablespoons unsalted butter, chilled
1 teaspoon vanilla extract
⅔ cup Chocolate Macadamia Nut Toffee (page 156), cut in small ¼-inch chunks, or about 8 ounces purchased toffee or Heath bars

Hot Fudge Sauce

A very rich, very thick, very fudgy, very slick sauce.

1. In a small saucepan, melt the butter. Remove from the heat, add the cocoa, and whisk until smooth.

2. Stir in the chopped chocolate, sugar, and evaporated milk. Bring sauce to a boil over medium heat, stirring all the while. Remove from heat at once and stir in salt. Cool briefly, then stir in vanilla.

NOTE

This sauce keeps nicely in the refrigerator.

YIELDS 2 CUPS

INGREDIENTS

5 tablespoons unsalted butter
1/4 cup cocoa powder, preferably Dutch process
2 squares unsweetened chocolate, chopped
3/4 cup granulated sugar
2/3 cup evaporated milk
Pinch salt
1 teaspoon vanilla extract

White Chocolate Clam Shell

Here is another spectacular presentation: a large, white shell that can hold cookies, candies, holiday bonbons.

1. The exterior of the clam shell should be as smooth as possible. Chip off any sharp ridges by placing the point of a screwdriver against the ridge, then tapping the handle gently but firmly with a hammer. When the shell is smooth, cover it over with 2 layers of plastic wrap, then 1 layer of aluminum foil smoothed down as neatly as possible and tucked under the rim of the mold to hold the plastic wrap in place. Lightly oil the foil. Line a baking sheet with foil and place the shell upside down on it.

2. Melt the grated white chocolate over hot water. Let the chocolate cool briefly, then smooth it over the foil with brush or spatula. Aim for a uniform ¼ inch thickness. (All of the chocolate will not be used.)

YIELDS ½ SHELL

INGREDIENTS

10-inch giant white decorative clam shell
¾ pound white chocolate, grated
Vegetable oil

3. Let the chocolate cool completely and harden (at least 2 hours). Trim excess chocolate from around the rim of the shell, then carefully lift off the real shell. Remove plastic wrap and foil.

4. Remelt the remaining chocolate and use it to re-attach any broken portions of shell. Using a pastry brush, work the chocolate over the interior of the shell until it becomes perfectly smooth. Let chocolate harden, then wrap and store.

5. After the shell is used, simply wipe out and store, covered, in a cool dry place. When finished with the shell, it can be broken into pieces and used in cooking.

NOTE

This makes a half clam shell. A truly spectacular presentation can be made by making 2 half shells and propping them open for display just like a double hinged shell.

Chocolate Soufflé Dish

*H*ere are 2 of the handsomest and most useful chocolate containers I know. I find it more practical to make 1 large rather than a multitude of small, individual containers, both because the single container takes less time and because it also allows a more spectacular presentation. The following chocolate soufflé dish can be filled and used several times. When it has done its serving duty, break up the chocolate and reuse it in cooking.

INGREDIENTS

*1 pound semisweet
   chocolate chips
Vegetable oil*

1.   One pound of chocolate will easily cover a 5-inch soufflé dish. For a larger dish, use 1½ pounds chocolate. It is better to have too much than too little chocolate. Melt the chocolate over hot but not bubbling water. While the chocolate melts, cover the outside of a soufflé dish with aluminum foil, and smooth the foil down and over the rim of the dish as neatly as possible. Lightly oil

the foil. Place the dish upside down on a foil-covered baking sheet.

2.   Let the chocolate cool just slightly, then, working rapidly, smooth it over the dish and down the sides. Spoon up the excess that tends to drip down and collect along the bottom rim. Keep spooning chocolate and smoothing it with a knife until the layer is as even (around ¼ inch thick) as you can make it. (There should be unused chocolate remaining.)

3.   Let the chocolate sit in a relatively cool place for at least 2 hours. It can be refrigerated briefly after 1 hour, but letting it harden of its own accord ensures the easiest unmolding. Resist the temptation to unmold the chocolate before it's time.

4.   When the chocolate is completely hard, lift up the bowl and remove the foil that folds into the mold. With a sharp knife, carefully

pare away the rim of the chocolate bowl until it is neat and even. Gently work out the ceramic mold, then peel off the foil from the inside of the bowl.

5.   If there are any thin spots in the dish, or if a portion of it has cracked, remelt the remaining chocolate and apply some from the inside to patch and strengthen the spots. With a finger or a palette knife, apply ridges of chocolate around the outside of the dish like the indentions on the ceramic soufflé dish. Let chocolate harden, then wrap the bowl and store until needed.

6.   To use, fit a layer of aluminum foil over the outside of the ceramic mold on which the bowl was formed. Fit the formed foil into the interior of the chocolate dish to act as an inner lining. After use, remove and discard foil and wipe the dish with paper toweling, so that it is ready for reuse.

Chocolate Autographs

If you sell your chocolate creations or give them as gifts, you will want to stamp your works with your own logo.

1. Melt some grated semisweet or couverture chocolate over hot water. Let it cool briefly.

2. Line a baking sheet with wax paper. Fit a pastry bag with a very small tube (⅛ inch), or make a bag from parchment paper and snip off a small scriptlike opening. Put the chocolate in the bag and press out solid rounds, ovals, or slightly scalloped shapes around 1½ inches wide. Place the sheet in the freezer briefly to set the chocolate rounds.

3. Pipe a raised rim around the edge of the chocolate wafers, then initial the center. Make up quantities of these and freeze them. To attach them, simply melt a drop of chocolate, press on the wafer, and let it

harden in place. These are effective on cakes and cheesecakes, and in boxes of candy.

My autograph looks like this:

Sources

*T*he 3 following mail-order sources provide among them all special ingredients and equipment that this book mentions.

FOWLERS OF DURHAM

Crystallized roses, violets, mint leaves, and ginger; rose and orange flower waters; almond paste; chestnut purée; Droste cocoa; pearl sugar *(pärl socker);* Almond Rocca; glacéed apricots and pears; pitted tart cherries; Tobler chocolate (white Narcisse, Tradition, and Extra-Bitter-sweet); Lanvin spécial pâtisserie chocolate (chocolat de ménage); Nestle's Peters couverture chocolates (bittersweet Gibralter, white Snowcap, milk chocolate Chatham, semisweet and unsweetened). Send for the Joy of Chocolate price list especially compiled for this book:

> Fowlers of Durham
> Brightleaf Square
> 905 West Main Street
> Durham, North Carolina 27701
> (919) 683-2555

MAID OF SCANDINAVIA

All shapes and sizes of baking pans including cheesecake pans; Silver-stone nonstick skillets; cookie cutters of all sizes and descriptions;

fluted ravioli cutters; nylon pastry bags and decorating tubes; stainless-steel mixing bowls; paper cake-pan liners; confectioners' gold foil; doilies; parchment paper triangles for making disposable frosting bags. General catalogue $1.

Maid of Scandinavia Co.
3244 Raleigh Avenue
Minneapolis, Minnesota 55416
1-800-328-6722 (toll-free)

WILLIAMS-SONOMA

Delicious Callebaut bittersweet couverture chocolate for finest candy making; Dutch-process Dark Jersey Cocoa by Guittard; porcelain pots de crème; heavy madeleine molds; stainless-steel Italian chocolate shaver for decorative curls; crystallized ginger; chocolate-coated mocha beans; wire cooling racks. Frequent catalogues featuring top equipment.

Williams-Sonoma
Mail Order Department
P.O. Box 3792
San Francisco, California 94119
(415) 652-1515

Index